THE HURTS CAN
BE REPAIRED

Robin Rochel Arne

THE HURTS CAN BE REPAIRED

Advantage
BOOKS

ROBIN (ROCHEL) ARNE

The Hurts Can Be Repaired by Robin (Rochel) Arne
Copyright © 2022 by Robin Arne
All Rights Reserved.
ISBN: 978-1-59755-710-8

Published by: ADVANTAGE BOOKS™, Longwood, FL, www.advbookstore.com

Library of Congress Catalog Number: 2022948115

First Printing: November 2022
22 23 24 25 26 27   10 9 8 7 6 5 4 3 2 1

Acknowledgements

This dedication is a reflection of faith. I trust in the Savior who grafts to me the needed inspiration and carries my thoughts forward so I may write with clear and hopeful management. God is the source of all I do and think. He has spoken and enlists my strength to piece together parts that make a whole.

I glean opportune meaning with Him with a mixture of true leadership where He is the coordinator. I do not claim to own the material I write. I give the credit to God alone. He is the one who inspires my speech on each page I document. His faithfulness to my thought process enhances the way I write and how I perceive what flows from the pen. Each stroke of the keyboard is new material presented by His hand. I teach through His direction. He favors and highlights His directives, so I realize what is necessary to place on the page. I am ever grateful for all He does with my life. We are a team, and we work as one. The balance Jesus offers is a magnet to my spirit. In Him, I find peace and harmony.

I also give credit to my mother, who has always supported my work, however it may look. She has been a sounding board to my heart and accepts my faults without question. Her grace has been a gift, and I welcome her input when I need encouragement. Her stance has always been to support and bless.

I am thankful for her every day.

Table of Contents

Introduction

Working by the light of day honors the baker while he prepares a loaf of bread. A craftsman must realize there is a time for harvest and planting. God works through one's heart, and He offers a reprieve if damage has been done. God realizes man needs His input in order to gain a blessed mental and hopeful insight that only He can offer. God is the understudy of any craft or design. He is the reason all plans unfold. You will find an abbreviated way to gain true character with His work, and a body of hope will unveil. God is the King, and He never misses a step. Through His guidance, one learns how to support a ministry or build a bridge. With His care, all hope of a future looks bright. Never judge what you do not understand. This is a principle where one learns that he is not the Creator.

God is instructional. He crafted the mighty grains of sand and created the heavens and the earth. No man can reproduce such things, nor can he build in any form of real power unless God authors him to do so.

Message One

Pain Is Not a Pupil

Each viewpoint is not always a suitable form of understudy. With God, there lies a plan and a purpose to bring to light the true nature of a man's soul. When heartache is present, fear can result in the display of the mind and the character it portrays. Crafting with a plan is a reliable way to move forward. Thanking the King in the process proves love is near and that the mind is willing to embrace the will of God for a brighter outlook and pattern of mature gain. A spirit is never without a loss when someone dies or sleeps in slumber due to a coma. A plan is inevitable when the circumstance is dire. Going it alone does not help a person gain a clear, hopeful mindset. When others build with care around your heart, you improve your sentiment and desire a broader body of others to perform some of the mental hardship tasks. This relates to a posture of goodwill or even a night at a neighbor's room and board.

This example shows the willing, opportune employment of another to the spirit and mind of a victim or one who is paralyzed by pain. Grafting to the King will enable a person to move into a sleep of a nature that ensures a mind can be attended to, even when there is no open pathway in the distant future. Embracing the way of Christ offers your mind the ability to bond with the knowledge that a better way is ahead. If you trust the Lord to build in your favor, you will realize there is fruit on every tree where the Lord plants His gospel form of truth. Considering that no man has ever been alone in the woods, since God is everywhere, the heart realizes that faith is important and should be looked at as a temple in the form of great witnesses and a true measure of a guidance counselor. Teaching allows the mind to form a path where the Bible is enhanced with a solid, stationary, divulged pattern where no fault can be found.

If you struggle with losing a loved one or a child's death, look at how God portrayed His love when He allowed His faithful child Jesus to hang in sheer pain and neglect of love. Where would man be if the great I Am is without a plan?

You can recognize God is the answer to all cares and hurts. He gifts the heart with a significant amount of endurance. All the while portraying to the mind that the work of the Lord is prosperous with a note of good measure and strength. A shadow casts a line in the way it dances and reveals a silhouette. The shade it offers is sure and safe, but there is no coverage against the rain or the snow.

The number of men is not a true witness of who the Father or His Son represents. It only tallies the amount of heritage God has created for His love of people. Teaching man to trust His person takes a toll on the individual who offers the love of God. But the bounty is an accurate measure of the faith a person has.

If you trust in the leadership of the Almighty, you will glean a true perspective that God alone is the Witnessmaker, and He can provide a path where true identity and love connect. Taking your partner's path does not necessarily make a life of good intent. Only the love of the Most High embraces a pattern where love and faith form a bond.

With Jesus, man can build and be restored. With Him, a plan never fails. God's character is not that of a thief. He is faithful and always a partner for the good of both He and His child.

A fake god never offers a plan where thoughts are bright and forthright. With God, authority is never a dark inspection or a depleted mental vision. God favors those who prepare and are willing to trust His lead. Pain is never a difficult undertaking when healing is offered through the testimony of Christ. With God, pain can be seen as a way to restore the mind and soul. If you lean into God's power, you will learn you can walk through fire and yet remain whole and pure. Take into account that you have trusted God to provide for you through the endeavors that were placed upon you. If you stand in faith and let God supply your needs, you will gain a modest return, but it will be balanced against the measure of good intent.

You will learn that your work rings true if you apply care and support. If you select to walk away and let your understanding guide your steps, you will lose the true face of God and be swept away in a lie. Be careful to display a righteous character because God is at the helm. He is not about to move you to a scale of weights where you lose footing or slip into the abyss. God offers a true connection to His person where honesty is a graft that places one in the corner of recognized hope. You will never lose your way if you trust the Lord to deliver your faith to His person and receive your prayer with courage. Planting your heart in the way it should go is a good formula, and a true way of thinking will ensue. Never doubt God will deliver. He is a Waymaker and a confessor of our sins. Because of Jesus's death, we can find hope and have a real plan of salvation to learn and be healed.

A person's walk is not measured by the steps he takes but by the way he presses forward. God leads and makes a formula that breaches the spirit and teaches it to love the forward way of Christ. Looking at what the Lord offers in the form of leadership and a tranquil host brings into play a mindset that produces a solid hope with care understood as a benefactor.

Relating to the King in such a way is an example of how good His connection to you is. You can tell your pains and needs to God without feeling like He will abandon you or walk away. God is not harsh, nor is He one to fend off an advance when someone calls to Him in their hour of need. God is at work building character along with solid motives that enable one to grow with a shield in place that catches the dark creases and irons them right and true.

Attempting to carry a load of pain on your own brings a battle from the depth of the mind and causes it to stumble. We, by ourselves, cannot supply the needed healing our hearts can embrace. The power of Christ brings true hope with a salve that can ease the master cut and restore the gain from a loss. Many feel rejected by friends or family. Even if it wasn't intentional, people could cause pain to others. With God at the helm, a heart can return to a state of pure grace with a balance of clear view where the pane of glass it holds is washed clean. This happens when there is a love for the Savior in our hearts and He embellishes it as a gravitational pull towards Himself. By His saving arms, we can stand against the dark envelope encasing our spirit. God teaches there is no real loss if He is our focus and partner in all we do. People pass away, but they never really leave our minds. Because our hearts miss the connection of the relationship we once had, that is why we suffer.

God is the salve that can enable our heart to grow a shield that encourages us in the memory department, and we gain hope that one day we will once again know their person as we do our own. Only those who love Jesus will find a pathway to heaven's gate. Anyone who embraces Christ as Lord is given a pass to the kingdom, and their spirit will be intact along with their special way of being. God does not rob one of his character when death takes one from this earth. He places it where it has chosen to be. Many think all go to heaven upon death. This is simply not true. The grave beckons to those who do not know the Savior. The people who have trusted Christ with their person are the ones we will meet again, providing the trust in Christ was genuine and forthright.

Traveling at the speed of light is not a design where faith is needed. The element of faith offers a true measure of insight grafted from the King, and He does not ever fall away from the fact He made all things that man understands.

Today people think they have wisdom and that they alone are the ones who suffer if a problem occurs. Little do they realize their mental breakage is due to not honoring what the word of the Bible has to say. The insight it holds can build a tower where the heart is at peace, and it finds a window to look out. Grafting with the knowledge that God the Father is the one who delivers a mental understanding where true bonding and harmony of the mind transpire is gained when a person endeavors on a path of righteousness.

Without the purpose of hope, one has difficulty gaining the way that leads to a clear field where the light is true. Speaking in favor of the Lord Almighty enables God to move freely in the range you offer to Him. If one never opens his heart toward the King, he never accomplishes much in the form of true worth. God never builds where He is not wanted. If pain is causing you to pull back and harbor hate due to an inflicted injury, whether it be a direct physical assault or spiritual wound, you will not relate to Christ, who is the healer of all hurts. You must step toward Him in faith and trust He will deliver your injury to the cross, where it will be made whole and no longer cause a sensitive embarkment against your person in the form of pain. A tingle of discomfort is a reminder, but that alone can build into a balm that eats at the core and makes it raw. With God, the pain is cured, but there remains the witness it presented.

The memory, however, will no longer control your motives or actions. A plan will supersede the doubt and anguish, and you will be refreshed in how you process thoughts. Your heart will entertain the idea that man is weak and can never hold up like the Father.

Man can't remain faithful through every trilogy, nor can he create a secure hatchway that leads to a pure, mental state of being. Only God can remain steadfast and complete in the desire He holds for His children. He alone is the one to trust with complete faith.

He is the Waymaker, and all His plans are right and true. He never steps in a wayward manner or makes a person stumble. However, He leads with a clear understanding of what must come first. He will branch your thought process and deliver you to a place of beauty. You must be willing with true intent, or you will not be able to embrace His offer of love, nor will you trust His leadership.

Today we need to embrace the fact that the Lord is a character where faith is pure within Him. He alone is the Waymaker. By His love, we find a faith that never fails. Through His workmanship, He made available upon His death we entered the ground of gifting. As a result, we need to accept the power put before us and utilize the gift He sent our way.

The cross message is contained in our spirit. We all know the truth of God even though we may not read the Book He granted us to know.

Our hearts still connect with the fact Christ is real. If you fight against this fact, you will not look at the hint your heart speaks; nonetheless, it will invite you to recognize Jesus is Lord. Accepting this as truth can be daunting for some.

However, many find this to be a long-lasting gift where they rest in the fact they are not alone. Comfort from the King is a gift that portrays kindness with workmanship that none can compare. The following verse is not spoken of to frighten but to enhance the heart with a love and a clear mental picture that God alone is the crafter who negates the negative and builds the positive at all times.

For the Lord is righteous, he loves justice; upright men will see his face. Psalm 11:7 NIV

The prophecy words of today are the same as before in the way they speak the truth. No Word of God is false. It all holds true, and it is secure in the format when embraced in the true form of God's design. He alone is the crafter and the manager. With His purpose before you, insight is presented and understood. You won't feel left alone in the dark, nor will you feel abandoned.

All the teachings of the Word are true, so that you can count on their enlightenment for wise counsel. Let the Savior be the Master to whom you offer your life. You will gain abundant knowledge and a wealth of hope that will guide your every move. God is faithful to His Word. He never fails nor steps aside from a true connection to His spirit. He showers the mind with clear and precise hope leading to a path of righteousness.

Each new phase of life offers insight that may enhance or decay a heart. Getting older brings a loss of youth, yet the mind is clear. However, some fall victim to disease and lose their faculties. It can be hard to watch a loved one engage in immoral behavior. We often think if we act in a certain way, we will gain friends. The fact we know many others does not add to our character. It simply determines the amount of praise we receive when we do well.

Conquering a multitude of directional plans is a goal in its own right. When one has friends to share the bounty with, a celebration of the spirit is a reward. Some keep close to the vest to whom they will give their thought process. Not all admire a wayward tongue that shares the news with everyone. If you spread gossip about others but aren't willing to share about yourself, you aren't reflecting a character of true goodness. However, many choose wisely and only offer fault when a certain number of character faults have been revealed. Having a few close friends builds a network where you stay silent and don't take on someone else's offense. Taking it upon yourself to share truths about another brings a loss to a person's perception of you.

People often choose to tell shameful aptitudes rather than the good qualities of others. This is the sin nature coming forth of its own free will.

When God hears us harshly speak about another, He does not draw close or share in the darkness. Remember, God is light, and He is the Waymaker. If you have been wronged, think about how it came to be. Were you honest in your relations, or did you present a lie? What was the true motive in gaining wealth when you purchased the property or built the home? Where did your heart lie? Was it under a sheath, or were you clear when you spoke about your ailments? Did you shower understanding, or were you deceitful?

People perceive in the manner that is presented to them. If a false presentation was put forth, you can't blame the individual for thinking you are better than you are. We all have faults, and they are enhanced when times of heartache ensue.

Life's riches are found in the pursuit of the Almighty, who is true and secure in His greatness. If you realize all of man is fallen, it is easier to comprehend none of us are worthy of atonement. We all need to understand that God made us unlike His person in that we fall short of the glory He represents. Our character is fallen because we are sinners. If you ever need a reminder of who to look to for recognition, God alone can bring about change. He is the one to follow. No man can compete with His person.

You are deceiving yourself if you think you are better off doing everything yourself. You can gain from another's perspective while learning how to form a bond and craft a skill set separate from your own. Shutting out a person is not an advantageous way to a quiet, solitary endeavor.

With personal gain comes a hope that others can learn from what you offer. Even though some prefer to work in a private setting, this does not stop you from helping someone else reach their dream. If you learn someone cares about the same cause instilled within you, open up and allow them to learn from your point of view or skill set. If we work together, we can learn from each other and achieve great things.

If you follow the stance of glorified religion in the case of opportunistic, material enhancement, you might find you have fallen short. You might realize sharing your knowledge shines more than a bank account of great wealth. Do you think you were the first to gain a witness by giving to a friend? Many have found favor by opening their hearts to the people who require their services or work knowledge. They may build a relationship based on their mutual interests. It is like teammates who bond together because they share a mutual goal. This factor is often misunderstood. If you consider not all people relate on the same level, you will learn there is always room for growth.

Not all will connect spiritually, but we can mature and come to understand that grace helps relationships. God does not leave one on a dark road with no options before him. He always provides a plan where one can shower another as well as himself, and he can learn how to calm the waters of differences between parties. Learning how to expand in the care department is a gift often overlooked by most. Keep watching for an open door to better acquaint yourself with another individual who needs assistance. You will gain an adept knowledge of how to pursue a plan, and you may offer insight that creates unity between yourself and the individual you are lending a gift of knowledge to.

The teaching of a plan is never the simplest way to help when the procedure is lengthy or complex. Leading by example and first-hand testimonies of God's goodness will have the best results. God is the expert, and He offers wisdom to all who ask. His Word tells you this is true.

For the Lord gives wisdom, and from his mouth come knowledge and understanding. Proverbs 2:6 NIV

The truncate keeps the blood from dispersing where it should not otherwise flow. In this manner, a wound can be repaired. God the Father is not to be fooled. When you are in pain, He hears your pleading even when you don't speak a word in His direction.

He can understand the sound of a heartbeat and when it is in distress. The pain of a love that no longer exists can bring pain that singes the mind and envelops the soul with an ache so deep you can hardly breathe.

Trusting that God is a healer brings with it the great hope He will alleviate what ails the package of darkness in your presence. God shadows you and delivers your mindset to a secluded place of worship. In the path of righteous endeavors, He discovers within you the motive and the wonder of where you can rest despite the detriment you face.

When you understand God the Father is a caregiver, you realize He is not able to grant a reprieve to those who do not accept Jesus as Savior and Lord. Without being redeemed, you can't expect Him to provide you with care when you aren't willing to adhere to His love in the first place. They work hand in hand and are a team of sorts. God offers a total commitment to the reality that you are His child even when you don't embrace this truth. A time of understudy where you reflect on the Word reveals His Lordship as true and rewarding in favor of love and unity. God's grace is ever before us. With Him, you find peace and a committed take on what is real and true, along with the knowledge God is human, yet not, but a force so great only He can match. You encounter the known parable God is genuine with a perfect opportune makeup that encompasses all in the form of great unity and survival of strength.

God's power is for all to see and is made available when one calls upon His name in a true call of worship. This is displayed when character meets the heart, and a bond of committed mindset unfolds. God hears every thought, and He is witness to all we think. You can't escape the realization there is none greater than God above. Only He is the Waymaker. He alone can bring a new way of thinking or a bridge where the pain is healed and removed from the body or spirit of individual parody. God formulates a pattern where growth is experienced and delivered to the needed area within a person so he may no longer be afflicted, wherein he is healed. How this process operates is by His hand alone. You can't force the issue. You must be willing to embrace the process and let God do the work. He never steps into an area He knows is not welcomed. So, if you suffer with no objective ground, place your discomfort in His grace. You will then form a clear way forward. God will remove your pain and suffering when He is the object of your thoughts. He is the one to give your attention to by reading His Word or speaking to Him throughout the day in prayer. You can do this simply by remembering that all you do is watched and seen by His makeup, so there is no holding back when a true offering of the heart is upon the table in your life.

God centers His person on the ground that is a welcome mat. Never does He infringe where He is not embraced as a whole. If you think you can muster a small token in His direction and expect to gain hope on any level, you will not see a reprieve, nor will you sense His spirit in your life in a personal manner or entanglement. God never speaks unless He is drawn by your spiritual connection to Him. He may reveal to you He is there, but He won't push His person in your direction without an accepted undertaking by you personally. He respects each individual's aspirations, whether it be with Him as Lord or as Him as an outsider in your life. But know no personal gain is without a measure of outreach to Him personally. He waits and accepts your decision-making; as a result, you alone are responsible for your own uplifting within His care.

A step forward is embraced if God sees a clear motive of true Lordship. He never invites His spirit to invade a mind or step on a person's intellect without a guidance counselor present. The universal magistrate of the mind is the Holy Spirit. If you have accepted Him into your heart, you have a way forward in the form of a union with the King. God operates through His presence with a clear incentive that unleashes the thought process to gain the upper hand with a directive of true character and leadership. God alone masters this process, evolving with a clear foundational longing where you continually seek to know God better through the process.

Seeking God teaches that man is a simple creature without leadership of his own. God prospers man's spirit to gain true character and enhances the mind with clear opportune realities. Teaching can be a tool for the heart, but with it comes a dark regional envelope in which man only knows so much. The Word of God teaches that God is all-knowing and all-seeing. This is the knowledge that He is real. There is no hindrance to a man's heart if he entrusts the true God of the universe, believing that there is none greater.

If this truth gains ground within the mind, it can be made a tool of strength. God, the caretaker for all man, is never in doubt or confused as man can be. Clarity is found at the helm of the most powerful there is, God the Father is a crafter in where He never fails or loses a step. He does not harm nor injure a party. That is not His way. He is fruitful and full of love for His creation, man.

God elaborates on the perfect creation He made. Though free will brings with it troubles all its own. God designed man to follow Him faithfully. When man gets outside this true connection, he slips and loses his way. God brings him back when a heart with a character that is true calls out to Him in faith.

Whether because of heartache or just simply because of faith, God will answer. He never leaves a person stranded or without hope; although it may appear that way, God is always there. Comforting and reassuring a person that He will never leave him or forsake his person. God crafts a love potion and brings the fruit of the vine with it. He is pure and just, with truth in abundance. He is always right with a directional latitude of grace, overpowering the doubt that wants to creep in. Trust the God of the Bible. He is a faithful character witness with grace and purity.

Today the sand is plentiful, and the Word written by God's hand is just as vast in that it holds nourishing attributes that cleanse the soul. God does not harbor an attitude in which none can pursue His person. He is diligent, and care is what He is made of. Looking at the many ways your Father builds a bond in the form of unity when one endeavors to read His manual for life is a token of grafted understanding where all gain and learn the true body of Christ. God reaches to you if you partake in the luxury of His skilled manual, and you retrieve a bountiful unity with Him on a personal level.

Never are you without a path to the forward building of love offered by the hand of love. God is great at building, and He makes available to all man the opportunity in a secure manner. The Lord is never one to cause harm or inflict a debt so that you cannot perform in a way that pleases your spirit. God offers each child the amount of care and hope that will lead to a trust in where He is honored.

People learn from one another, but through this process, they are not always granted the knowledge needed to be a great master. Many hold back when teaching others to cause a dependency on more instruction. A true prophet would embellish only the Word of God and give only what was spoken to him by His Lordship. If you truly believe you know enough to grant others favor with your insight, this is a gift you need to embellish.

Don't be afraid to secure monetary gifting through the operation of the grant of knowledge. This is how economics work. We learn from one another and pay for the privilege of learning a skill. If you relish the hold you have on your wisdom, you aren't a person of character. God desires us to share what we learn from a book or personal instruction. Talents are to be adhered to in such a way that they reflect a true signature of opportunity investment into another's way of being. Granting our operational goods and services brings to the playing field a decent and honorable, manifested stronghold to the character we present.

With the purpose of growth in mind, one can begin to elaborate on where he should place his trust. Offering to others simply to invest with a pure motive of help at the center of the offer is a true character that enhances the spirit and gifts it with a plan of good measure. God the Father never doubts a mind that is centered on His attributes and knows how to be a reflection of that. The honorable way to bring another into the realm of true mental gain is by offering what you know to do in a manner of grace. Not all investments are for the benefit of just the purse. If you truly need an income, then a fee is appropriate for the gift of knowledge you will share. Conquering the fear that another will steal your profits or ideas is not something the Lord instills into the mind. When you offer your skill set, know that many only desire to understand the process, not to duplicate your way of creating or your management style when a project is being formulated. Today's understudy is an example of how a person learns from the written knowledge another shares through a book format. I don't preach nor offer seminars for others to learn from my thought process. I suggest that people know how to communicate their private gifts better and share what they know without fear of losing their recognition or their talent to others. No one person ever has complete control of a talent. Man shares the same skill set with many. God designed us to be unique. However, many of us are given the same reprieve of skills. How we use them is what separates us from one another. Our drive tells the tale of how much experience we have applied to the growth and mature way of expression we hold at our fingertips. The way the body moves or bends is not the same for all, nor is the thought process the same. God has granted us favor so we can reflect on our way of being.

Offer today what you would enjoy from another. Be free with your knowledge and adhere to the fact God makes us all unique. Trust God will organize the needed standpoint where you can balance free will with the desire to advance the kingdom of God. Consider that your mind delivers its gravitational advantage as to who you should serve and to what extent. We often share what we learn with the people closest to us. Outside our personal boundaries, we are hesitant to offer others capital gains or enhancement of true honor-ship. With God, we are all the same. We all reflect His care, and His true love is showered to us from above.

The table with a dinner setting is beautiful when china is on display. All the pieces hold beauty in which they reflect the patterns imprinted upon their embodiment. Each cup is simple yet fully decorative. The plates hold a meal, and they support food with a balance when one nourishes the center and goes out from there. Each message of true inspiration is a gesture where God is the one to perform a solid unity with His people. You can understand this more clearly when you look to scripture. Each passage holds true in its form and written display.

> *He replied to him, "Who is my mother, and who are my brothers?" Pointing to his disciples, he said, "Here are my mother and brothers. For whoever does the will of my Father is my brother and sister and mother." Matt. 12: 48-50 NIV*

Message Two

God's Light is Faithfulness

Hearing God speak is not always presented in the form of a voice. He moves in many formulas, and He often reveals the true nature of His plan in the form of growth. Understanding that God will work with you on a motion ensures that you understand He alone is the crafter. He never works in such a manner that all evidence is hidden or placed out of sight. When God is working, He is secure in the manner that unfolds as He is the Waymaker and His steps are true and correct. God provides many resources for you to advance in your area of study. He favors a plan where not all can be witnessed by one individual. He involves a multitude, so many can reap and sow a harvest. If you think you are the one to bring a plan to a heightened bridge, remember the cross was a masterpiece.

God did this to enlighten the care He made available, but even then, many were involved. Suppose you desire a pure method of unity look at where God has placed your work. Are you waiting for Him to ensure you with a more solid unity so you can adhere to the proper placement of His witness, or has your mind desired a singular trial or gain? Where is the bounty to be granted? Are you in need of more enhanced ability, or would the aid of another be beneficial? God moves where He is welcome. He does not offer the way to success when only a dollar sign is what the motive or goal reflects. If you enjoy the love of God and desire for another to gain this gift, you're probably looking for the door of the workman where the plan is for many to attain. Perhaps you alone are the one with the dream. God can still do great things with just the faith of one individual. If you are willing but have not had the path forward, look at what is needed. Would the joining of hands be beneficial? Are there others working toward the goal you have? Do you seek out any who would enjoy the gains you hope to have? There may be insight you can offer if you look at who also builds in the area you do. Still, there is the possibility that God will make you an example of strength simply because you alone are the one who stepped forward and offered your heart to Him in faith.

If God leads you in a direction you recognize as good and pure, rest in the truth. He alone knows what you need. Surrender your status as a believer and set aside the desire to go it alone. God will provide the material, strength, and hands to help harvest and plant. God enjoys when He can be displayed by many. Your will to serve Him can be shared and witnessed by many, even if you are the one with the goal of the adventure. God works in such a manner that one brings into the fold the others who will enjoy the opportunity of sharing the message of God's character, and His direct nature will be witnessed. If the timing has not been revealed, know God is the Master. He can bring into action a quick encampment, and unity can be underway. Building with someone you have never known may develop out of a desire to be near the King. A united heart will register, and an awakening will spring onto the scene. Trust God for a guided outlook and a perspective of clear unity with His way of operating will unfold. This does not mean God will take away your hopes or build a nonrelated material outreach in you. It simply initiates a better way forward. God is at work building and creating. He never sleeps or slumbers. In this revelation, you can gain a real mental hope that God will never tarry. He won't foreshadow a plan or make it disappear. He will move and bring into light how one is to proceed. His favor is good. He is a Master at what He does.

Each supplier of goods carries, in their case, knowledge of how to go about a real individual gain in the form of relational gain and opportune marketing. If you alone can harvest and store rewards, this is a benefit. Many have learned that to move further in the marketing division, they must first understand where to place their offerings and how to appease those who desire what they process. The formula for gaining profit is easily realized when there is a return or profit emitted once the transaction of relational cooperation has transpired. If you have been offered the intellect of how to manage profits, you are in the know as to where to invest. Many do not comprehend that their goods can bring a balance to another's needs. Market your good character by being diligent and honest when you engage in the transaction of business relations. If you cheat or harbor ill-gotten gains, you will lose the respect of those you robbed, and no character will be seen. God is not one to forget your goodwill, nor is He one to step aside when a wrong has been emitted. He will replace your purse if it is stolen, and you will not hold only empty air. When the right measure has been rewarded, both parties of a business proceeding will inherit what is rightfully theirs. Even when someone claims what is not his, he may still gain rewards, but they will not be a witness to true ownership. They will represent a theft, and all will know at some point what transpired. God reveals a loss in the form of accounting or ledgers. Somewhere the theft will come to light. You may not inherit your standing in the realm of God's grace, or you may find you have lost the capital in another form. Either way, a balance will be brought forth to repair the damage. God will make right what is wrong and set things in proper order. Never will He manufacture a negative when a claim is not rightfully placed where it truthfully is set to be displayed. God can build in many forms, whether through a unified caretaking or a quiet release of funds. Know God is the one to offer hope with true grit and forthright personal investments that bless the mind and show gratitude.

A look at the plan one is witnessing is a signal that hope can be found for the pursuit of knowledge that offers a solid unity with great admiration and true, opportunistic, mental clarity when God is the one at work. He provides the door where man is to go forth. He alone is the one to offer a guide in where the light of clear view is apparent. A shadow may occur if it reflects where you have placed your trust. Are you following along the way the Savior would have you travel? Have you taken the road of clear and distinct recognition that God alone is the Master who carries with Him the knowledge of how to proceed? Do you rely on Him alone, or have you begun to harness the desire to follow man? Where does your hope and faith lie? Are you given to doubt where you think you will never have what your perspective has in mind? If this is the case, take to heart what the Word of God speaks of concerning how to find peace. Look at the way God speaks to the mind and heart. He portrays a true love for His people.

> *O Lord my God, I take refuge in you; save and deliver me from all who pursue me, Psalm 7:1 NIV*

God is forthright and pure. He does not carry a torch for deceit nor offers false dreams of no value. If you partake in a plan that has no direct gain in the form of growth of the spirit, where is the purpose of its implementation?

Would it reflect in a positive outcome of a solid character and a total, complete package of great unity with God above? Without the purpose of bringing glory to God the Father, there is no good measure in any work put forth without His approval or character witness. God alone is the example we need to follow. He is the one we all should glean insight from. When we follow His direct way of thinking and being, we form a union in which our utmost best is portrayed in the developmental stage of all that is good and true. Even our sleep patterns will conform to the Most High. This is a result of a connection between our will and His.

Christ is the example we follow to pursue His Father in faith. He is the one who represents the intellect and the care of a true, moral witness, thereby knowing the God we trust is ever faithful. If you follow the King, you will learn He is the way. You will discover that He not only saves the soul from death, but He also rears the mind into a clear, precise aptitude and trust. When one offers the gift of unity with God, it results in a positive growth experience. God delivers to His people the way to move ahead. He does not lead without first securing a measure of a unified belted plan. He will enlighten a person with the skill to go about the benefited step in a move of great strength and secure footing. If you are in doubt, consider the notion God has you in a holding pattern. During the process, He will guide you with new material so that your spirit recognizes His plan is moving forward. It may not be as you thought it would be, but that doesn't mean you aren't on track. God often has a better way of doing things that we can connect with; if an outlook of more intent is what you feel, judge how you have proceeded so far. Can you understand the process you have partaken of? Do things align to a future-guided pathway? If you have the intellect that what you hold at this time is good and secure and it would gift others, then you are following a witness of astute hope that embellishes upon the union with God. Take yourself out of the equation. Where would things rest if you were not offering your skill set? Would it collapse and be lost in its formation? If you are vital to the growing expenditure, you may need more focus. Look at where your steps have led. Do they align with a normal progression in the way they present? Is the goal for Christ and His person? Have you taken what you know to do and applied all you have in the way of faith and technical expertise? Then muster up the courage to claim what lies ahead when the gate is no longer blocked. Courage builds a mighty gateway where God can use our makeup to further His claim that He is real. Be a standard of true commitment. Harvest the grain where it may be found. Faith secures in our mind that God alone is our creator and that His love for us is ever present. Trusting Him to lead builds a unified mental gain where we grow closer to Him as a whole.

God favors the ones who trust His leadership and continue in faith to serve Him in love. There are many ways to offer God your heart on a platter of true witness and opportune methods of clear faith. We can serve others and meet them where their need is, or we can step into the ring of teaching and offer our skill set. With God at the helm, we can build a solid mental lead where all around us we are seen as people of mature knowledge or grace. Each person God has created knows a skill or trade in one form or another. God has granted to all of man, even the individual with handicaps can produce in some form or another a grace in which he is capable of relating to others. In this manner, he can offer connected relationships that absorb the dark mind and bring it into hope. A simple gesture of kindness provides an opportune time to embellish who the Savior is and what He represents can be witnessed in your conversation. Each article written by a person can be studied and seen as either a real statement in where truth is offered, or it can be a slight against the person God is. Little is represented in the way of mankind and what he is capable of unless it is a textbook that is a manual of some influence in a particular field of study. When God is discussed on the page of any body of writing, His reflective nature may or may not be displayed in a manner of true integrity.

Teaching is never forgotten, whether it be from man or God. What you know can be recalled even if it has been many years since you studied it. What we glean from our study shows who we follow or bond to. God is the Waymaker. He never leaves a mind in a hole of darkness or deep depravity. God allows man to lose footing if he chooses to leave the comfort of His arms, but He does not perform the act that causes the separate void. If you are sure that God is your Savior, do you spend quality time in His Word of good measure? Do you prepare for the day by first engaging with His person? Are you connected to Him spiritually at any given point in the day? Would you miss your reading time if it were removed from the calendar you follow as a guide for time management? These measures assure a bond of growth in which you and the Lord build a treasure of unity that no one thing can come between. You are protected by the hand God places around your person in the manner of love and honor.

The love God offers is found in the way He portrays His character through the Word He presented by the men who followed Him in faith. Each was privy to His instruction, and they served Him in the form of a witness. The member body they offered is solid in its design. Many have fallen prey to the idea God would not use a study manual to teach man who He is. They believe God would work in another fashion. How God chooses to deliver His goodwill is not for our understanding. We are to embrace what His standard is and accept that He alone knows how to teach our minds the truth of who He is, the all-knowing individual body that none can compare or completely box in. God's talent is far superior to ours. We forget that He made the universe and all it contains. God is always a step ahead and never leashes a bounty that He can't fulfill. Considering the Father you know, would you expect Him to follow another's lead? Our timetable is separate, and our management style is weak in comparison. The Lord is a great manager. He leads and displaces the perfect order for growth where all are tied to His person. This creates order and strength where none existed prior to God incorporating His grace and character upon our hearts. God never distinguishes His great power as an instrument where He hurts the individual He is trying to aid. He will allow a perfect balance of His administered mindset with the implantation of man's thought process to act as an adhesive between the two.

The character one portrays is connected to his interpretation of who he desires to represent. Whether it be the Lord Jesus Christ or Satan, the choice is his alone. God does not hinder a mind or control the thought process. He lets man configure what he desires, and then He steps forward or back depending upon the faith put forth. An ounce of good intent can carry one over the threshold and into the arms of the loving God. If you ever find your heart broken, God can heal what ails you. He is the caretaker of mankind, and His embodiment guarantees a solid reprieve if you allow Him to act on your behalf. He will mend the pain and give it a fresh new plan where He is the focus. As a result, you will have an intent of wholesome fortitude characterized by the Savior Himself. This allows one to understand that He alone is worthy of his favor. Loving is not a rejection when another steps away. It is a staple where a statement can be heard that a breach does not affect the bond one has for another. If a person has taken the lead and is no longer a witness to good character, that is the time to walk toward Christ. He will deliver an appetite that feeds on His power, subjecting a soul to a formula in which all thought processes are pointed to the one in control. God does not allow man to worship outside of His person in such a way that God is not the center of one's heart. In the case of a false god, the Lord will not intervene and will allow a depraved individual to be consumed in his own right. If a choice to pursue a false witness is what you desire, God will allow it, and He will not remove your position as His child until you have lost your way completely with the last rejection of Christ. God hears man, and he knows who trusts in His person. He showers understanding to those who accept Jesus as Lord. Without this admission, one is not truly connected to the spirit of God. God supplies the needed gift of salvation. All you need to relate to this truth is the belief God loves you enough to pave the way for you to be with Him personally. Many fake their belief, but God alone hears the heart. You can't hide a real love of God. If you do, where are your courage and strength? Is God not worthy of your effort to share Him? Is He not the one who offers eternal life? Should this not be your focus and hope for all mankind? When one pursues the Lord, he finds his heart is no longer tied to doubt. He is given the knowledge that God is most valuable, and there is no greater truth than Him alone.

Taking into account God alone is the one to control how a man gains entry to heaven's gate, we need to expect there to be some form of opportune way to get there. Should God have made another route? How would it look to you? Where would the power come from? Where would the state of affairs you design lead? Would you offer man the option, or would you judge on what they have done to glorify your person alone? Would you have offered the choice upon death? What seems just to you is only your mental ability to understand the way things appear to you specifically. Others may have a different point of view. What then? How does one distinguish one's aptitude to gain a secure foothold if there is no real effort to create a unity in which man and God are united? How would you handle this objective? Did God not make the best formula for man to know Him by?

A choice offers a blank slate in which man can begin a new path toward a goal. If God is at the helm, He can build with a purpose and a plan of goodwill. In the event man thinks he knows best, there will arise problems outside of the scope of good graces. Teaching brings one to the frontline by leading where others cannot proceed. Each established forefront was obtained because there was a body standing at the ready to fight for a cause he believed in. With God, much is understood before the entanglement of a fight ensues. If a character is sound, it will step back and resist the object of possession. No one thing is more valuable than how God portrays His symbolism of good merit. If you are about to branch into a new field, look where it will lead you. Will the ground material support your mental view of ownership? Would you want others to know you invested in the property, be it realism or spiritual? Where is the plan of good intent? Is it front and center with a true work of good style and merit as its home and local energy? In this, I attempt to underline that God alone is the one to follow and pursue. Many have fallen because they put their faith and trust in an object, be it man or goods of some kind, and then learned they have fallen prey to deceit. God does not bring His insight into the ring of lies like Satan does. He does not offer great wealth at the sacrifice of good moral inhibition. You can stand on this true measure or believe the opposite, but with God, all things are right and true. There can be no other way with Him. His makeup is unique, and it supports all good things.

God is the way to what is important in life. He is bound by a true, moral witness that conforms to His will. You can't control how God operates, but you can learn from it. With Him, insight is given, and a balance of unity is built. Watch the world around you. Who stands strong against adversity? Does the wind blow, and then man falls short? If one pursues the love of God and truly desires to be His friend and partner, he will acknowledge God knows all. His life will adhere to what the Lord speaks, and he will lead with moral justice.

The teaching of the Lord is a way to negate the world with a clear view. It is masterful with the right training in true character building. When one follows the path of the King, he bears witness at the same time as offering others the knowledge of where to turn in times of trouble. Always knowing where to look for faith and guidance will represent the light of God at all times. A person who trusts the Savior will relinquish the desire to step outside His instruction. He will realize the right way is better and pursue the way forward with the intent to honor the God of all. If you're looking for a healing, understand God is the only way to receive such a gift. He is the Waymaker and the true balance within the heart. He is the offering where one finds peace and security. With God, the formula for branding the whole of the pain is removed and, in its place, is a pure relish of good measure. Hoping for insight from an outside source will only bring another's point of view into play. It may be right and true, or it may offer a lie where you develop a loss of clarity. With God, the viewpoint is on track and doesn't veer to the left or right. In Him is found the purpose for life. You may have pain due to a forgotten vow, but you know God is in control. He can ease the loss with His person, and you will gain liberty where you no longer hold tight to what is gone. An offering of faith is what brings God close, so invest your heart toward His excellent character. It will bring a solid, opportune way to harvest the grain of the mind, thereby offering the memory hope and a future where truth is always on the perimeter of self-reflection. In the manner of never holding fast as a result of another acting out of despair, reach into the gateway of hidden hope. By the favor of the Savior, all mankind is free. If pain is all you see, reflect on the cross and how great the pain was that Christ Himself endured all because He desired you as His child. You will find no greater love or commitment than Jesus to you.

Embellish your heart in the direct course of action needed to acquire a more solid drive toward knowing who God is. This will ensure you are gaining in the way of good instruction. Teaching from the Bible will grant an understudy in which your heart embraces the knowledge God is true and good. Never in the Word is God spoken of as deceitful or as a liar. God never operates in the zone of sin. His makeup is only fair and just, so why not commit and offer your love to Him? He has done this for you with only a simple gesture of good faith as the bill. God ties His heart to yours when you profess that He is Lord, and with it comes the unity you desire within your spirit. The void will seal, and you will then know the promise of God for all time.

When the Lord speaks, a heart hears the gentle knowledge it is gifted. When man tries to learn who the Father is and what His character is, God will supply him with the necessary incentive and the know-how of where to engage his thought pattern. God does not overreach the mind, nor does He step on a person's will. He puts forth the gift of knowledge and then allows man to digest what is truth to him. Whether man has decided to follow the dark and embrace lies is a way God allows man to proceed, but if man decides the light is where he desires his heart to rest, then God moves forward and offers His love and care to enable man to reach deeper into His person. God is gentle in His rearing. He moves in a delicate manner, and He gifts the spirit with a true envelope of hope. That is why you can move freely when you trust and favor the way of the Lord. All who desire a life of true character will indulge in how God operates. He won't seek another once God has been found. All the negative pronouns will pass from the mind, and a clear assumption will partake the spirit with a balance of integral, opportune meaning. God is always a Waymaker. His plan will never be of a hurtful or destructive hardship. He gifts with fruit that is real and formal in its display. He is subtle when it comes to leading. He gives the option for man to embrace all He is with the guidance of a clear manifestation of love. No other can perform in this multitude. By accepting who the Father is, you gain a way of mental knowledge that forms a graft in which your bond with God is solid. However, it takes a commitment to Him personally for growth to bring into play a stand and an absolute joy in which man accepts Christ is the true King. Knowing Jesus is real and believing He is the righteous Savior are separate in their course of action.

God is holy, and He engages with a love that holds secure the heart of any individual who recognizes God as a character of integral design. He does not formulate a late way of being. All His mannerisms are a solid representative of good moral standing. You won't find a loss when you move in His direction. Your approach to life will change, and you will understand there is hope in all you do and perform.

The cross is the motivation for love because it holds the plan for man to gain entry to the gate of heaven. Without it, we all would be lost. Even those who live as good caretakers for others would not be delivered without the plan of salvation. God is direct when it comes to His love offering. His Son was offered as a sentiment of true, moral goodness whereby the escape from hell was granted. Only Jesus can bring a person to His Father. He alone is the way. Many have sought to prove this false, but none have proven God is not faithful. None can master that deception. God protects the ministry of His name, and He leads the willing to His center of grace. The blood Jesus shed is full of forgiveness because it holds the power of His person within each drop. God alone could master the needed undertaking of making man acceptable through the mechanism of His leadership. With the cross, man can follow the Savior to a place of beauty and forthright honor where all are pure. Only the God of the universe could build a connected stream of faith in which He and man could be united. God's power carries man to Himself in a gentle belief where He and man can reside as a team. God offers with this purchase of trust a way forward in the manner of redemption and a connected bond for both parties to know one another. Deciding to have faith in the one called God is a factor that brings with it a commitment to trust and adhere to the Word of God. You can't just coast in life if God is who you serve. The embellishment of a favor offers the knowledge that in that grant is the reciprocated understanding a return will come.

God is not only all-knowing, and He is a measure of unity. This takes place when reading of the Word is undertaken. If you take time to read what the Lord has offered, knowing who He is, you show you favor a walk with Him. If Christ is your focus, you will adhere to study time with Him and lean into Him during the process. Talking about the Lord lifts up His name, but when you show Him attention through the pages, He provides in the Bible, you express a genuine belief that He is the creator of all things. It is similar to a love letter from a friend or relative where you are acknowledged and trusted. It graces the soul and speaks to Him directly that you are committed to Him and dine on His greatness.

Speaking with the Savior based on trust is a connection to where the Lord is at work, enlightening your thought process. He corresponds in a manner of true power, and it is released to your person in the form of pure acknowledgment that God is genuine and an upholder of clear mental design. The Lord is magnificent and leads with a pure outlook, character, and strength. Scripture teaches us we are His bride, and He loves us with great care.

> *For the husband is the head of the wife as Christ is the head of the church, his body, of which he is the Savior. Ephesians 5:23 NIV*

Message Three

God Supports Man as His Own

God's character is quaint, and it is not harsh. God alone can speak subtly, drawing a person to His direct, mental gain for them. God embellishes on the true character one holds and implements it into a stronger reflection of Himself. God does not harness the mind; He polishes it to become a sound witness of the truth. When God is at work, you will gain the knowledge that He alone is the Master and caretaker of your inner being. When you trust in His person, you will favor a path of pure, gross management. You won't look to a false appreciation; instead, you will strive toward a goal of unity with the Maker. His craftsmanship is pure, so you won't find a false dimension when applying yourself to His leadership. God offers a plan that is holy and one that is forthright. He never steps out of bounds, nor will he engage in deceit, so you may know you are safe when you seek His person. There is none like the Father but Jesus alone. He is set apart in how He proceeds forward with care and a humble mental way of being. God is honest and true. He is blessed with knowledge and delivers hope on a board of distinguished maintenance. He does not slip or lose His way and never takes part in a lie. He will bring you a design element where faith contrives the mind and builds a reflective hope that God will deliver on His promises. In the Word of God, you will find many examples where He offers a plan with the intent of guiding a thought process to success. If you apply your efforts toward His leadership style, you will understand a way forward in the manner of gifted intellect.

Reaching toward the goal of hope is a mental way to proceed with grace and an opportune makeup of love because God is the designer of all good things. He creates a mindset in which love is the focus for a person to learn true faith in His person. All love comes from God above, whether it be toward the Master or a loved one on earth. However, the enemy also interjects a false draw toward an unrighteous, entertained thought process, and he will cause you to fail in a marriage or good workmanship. He does not desire for you to have a successful lifestyle, nor does he want people to remain faithful in their commitments to one another. God never focuses on a person's faults, so if this is forming within your mind, invest in the purpose of hope. Look at what God has to say concerning leaving a spouse or breaking a bond with a partner who has built a foundation for an investment of returns where you are united as a team. God will bring you a relief package, and you will then learn real understanding. He showers those who trust His lead. Forgiveness is always on the table if you have forsaken a marriage, but first, there must be repentance. If you desire a real relational bond with God, deceit must be cast away and washed under the blood of Christ Jesus.

The Lord is the crafter of all things true. In Him is a way forward. He builds with character, so you understand He will never fail you. Stepping away is what brings a loss. If you are anchored in the Word and stay planted in prayer, you will witness strength, and sure-footedness will transpire. A capital gain will be measured by the hand of the Lord. If He deems it necessary to grant an income for your effort of investment, He will do so but don't assume that will happen when doubt or inhibitions of the soul are present. God leans into a person when He is called to. If you trust the Lord but still can't commit to the fact that He is all-powerful, then you aren't letting Him move in your favor. You may have built a reputation and made a name for yourself, but where is the eternal stand if all was done in vain? If you focus on the care God can offer, then trust Him to provide your needs in a manner where your hope reflects this trust. Preparedness is an option and a good management style, but solely relying on your abilities will not gain you favor upon judgment day. A harvest of a solid endeavor is fruitful but understand the Lord is the one to embellish a heart and make it whole and complete. If pain is a way of life due to an injury, God offers His ability for healing or endurance. You are never alone or without His guidance. Look in the Bible and learn who you serve.

To keep me from becoming conceited because of these surpassingly great revelations, there was given me a thorn in my flesh, a messenger of Satan, to torment me. Three times I pleaded with the Lord to take it away from me. But he said to me, "My grace is sufficient for you, for my power is made perfect in weakness." 2 Corinthians 12:7-9 NIV

The temple of God is within our person. We are what holds the Holy Spirit intact. It is by our feeble mindset that He is embraced or rejected. We alone are the ones to obtain eternal grace or lose life to a dark embodiment of pain. Satan has placed a mark of hate on those who have chosen outside of the walk with God. He obstructs the mind with lies and deceit. He brings forth pride, and an object of deception always formulates when he is the one in control. It is easy to assess the King from the dark side. God is always a great deliverer of a true mindset. He does not bring any deceit or longing for a free, get-out-of-jail card. There needs to be a commitment from a person of Christ for true merit and wisdom to unfold. Taking the attitude God loves all is wise, but with it must be the understanding that God makes a way for grace to be present so you and He can meet as one. Without the understanding of the Savior, you will never hold fast to the fact God alone is the reason anyone makes it to the land of prosperity called heaven. God's house is plentiful in the way of hosts and willing spirits of true adoration toward His person. If you think He will attend to you professionally, then allow you entrance to His place of honor without the benefit of calling on Jesus for salvation, you have not heard the message God offers in His Word.

Teaching others to know who the Savior is will result in grace being given to future generations. Staying silent only brings a loss to those you encounter. Anyone can give a testimony and lead others to the knowledge of who Jesus is as Lord and Savior. But the fact of professing must also follow the revealment. If one only talks about the Lord but doesn't come to the knowledge grace entered the scene, the realization that God alone is the one who gave the witness and secured the body to Himself will never be a focal point. When faith enters the picture, grace is released, and a bond is formed where two become one. God the Father and His Son meet the heart, and a true commitment transpires. Following Christ is an example of pure faith. No one has seen the face of Christ though many have felt His person within them. When He speaks, a solid foundational thought enters the mind, and you can relate that it is pure. If an intruder enters, does not the homeowner recognize him as false? If you are in doubt, look at what the Word of God teaches. There will be a clear, distinct plan when God is the one speaking. There won't be a façade of lies or grand endearments of false praise. God grants wisdom with perspective. He is methodical with purpose. He will give a person a goal with a plan to achieve it. It may come in steps, but you will see a positive outlook with a lead of goodwill before you.

The God you pursue will lead to a life of good measure or a dark channel with no opening toward the rich ground of faith where man and God become united. Taking the measure of faith and acting toward a harvest in good endeavors brings with it the request to know God's person in a better reprieve and hope. With God, you will grow and learn who is the real King and where He can be found. Facing the realization that man is not who he desires to be, grants the witness that only God can bring change. Only He can interject the true means by way of faith to interlope a plan of good measure. When man thinks he alone is the one with great gifts, he loses the true understanding that God is the Waymaker. The true character offered from the hand of God is stable and unique in that no other has ever been able to benefit from a true call to grace. God provides this through His Son, the Lord Jesus Christ. Gaining in the way of capital rewards does not make one steadfast or solid when it comes to a clear set of moral values. Many have gotten wealthy on the backs of others with little offered in the way of return to another's hands. When you seek only to gain in a material manner, you lose the footing offered by the witness of good character. You can multiply financially, but it must transpire in the form of pure intent. Working with an honest approach breeds the market of solid staples in that the mind is part of the pattern of growth. If a calculated pattern of injustice is presented somewhere, the truth will be revealed, and all will blow by in the wind. A bank account may bring a secure undertone but not a true witness of good, moral hygiene. The envelope of unity will not be present; without this process, the value of what you have worked for is not real. Each little step toward prosperity must be accompanied by the humble attribute that God alone is the caretaker of hearts and minds. Crafting outside of His glory leaves the balance of little to no prosperous revenue in the eyes of His judgment. On judgment hour, there will rest the avenue you sought to follow and how you went about the course of action to secure your wealth. It will be tried by the fact of whether you offered a hand to the needy or the forsaken. If you decided to invest in the growth of many, the reward will be stable and sure. We don't know the day or the hour, but we can know the season and the account of our life. If we reflect on how we served the needy, we will realize our foothold is narrow or wide. Today you can begin a new form of unity by sharing your gifts and offering your attributes in the form of genuine strength for the witness of God. This will ensure your work is placed on the pedestal of true greatness instead of the dead margin of gain many believe is fruitful.

The truth is told by those who invest in the way man operates or lives. All of the work one does in a lifetime is reflective of who he believes the true God or holder of his heart is. If you trust the Lord, you will work for the glory of His fashion in that you won't teach a false narrative. There will be a constant love for His person, and you will think on ways to offer others the hope you have found through the love of the sacrifice the Savior made at Calvary. Understanding God is real yet set apart by the greatness He portrays enlightens the mind that He alone can craft a way forward toward the love each man desires for himself. God does not offer a fake mixture of unity in where He never harbors the mind in the form of deceit. When God is the operator, you gain a perspective on where His grace is real to you, and you dine on the witness it offers. Going it alone offers little in the way of hope. Trials come that hinder the outlook and cause one to lose faith. If God is near, you can operate knowing He fights the battle for you. He never leaves a heart once it has accepted Him as Lord. It is a lifelong endeavor where your spirit will always be acquainted with Him personally. How strong that bond is depends on whether you invite Him to expand upon your relationship with His presence and your faith intertwined. God the Father is careful to whom He offers a leading role. Many pastors have risen up and made a significant plan of forward witness their goal in life. This form of telling who God is may not be your style or calling. Many tell the tale of true recognition in other maneuverable manners—each one designed to spread the Gospel in its unique mannerism.

If you believe the power of the Lord is a gift and that He acts with love, you will adhere to the fact that God is always gracious and always at your side. God is perfect and true, and His need for His people to relish His person is not a hardship to His character. It simply displays His love in a manner of great developmental enhancement and notoriety. The God known as Savior is Jesus. He is the Waymaker and a true ornament of greatness. You can't describe such a King. We must believe He is real. The power He affiliates to is from the one above, the God of the universe, and then some. He is the way we may gain entry to the sacred home of heaven, the place God rests His heart. Trust the Lord, and He will grant you understanding as to where to search for more of His character. In this, you will learn how to practice the teaching and gain a moral way of being. The shadow of truth will be ever-present, and you will gain more intellect while connecting with God Himself. The power of the Word brings one to the throne, and the heartbeat of Christ is witnessed there.

The teaching of the Word is not a shallow thought process. It is secure with a balance and a unity in which one entertains the connected honor of knowing the Lord and His person is revealed. If you lose a team player, is not the loss felt and recorded within the spirit of the body remaining? This is the process you can relate to, as God is also connected to the mind and body and the spirit within. He formulates a distinct opportune narrative in which all people have the desire to gain an understanding of His great person. If you seek another source for your desire, you will lose face and fall deeper into deceit. The pain of heartache will ensue, and you may not realize you have lost the connected unity God instilled within your spirit, thus resulting in a further demise against your own true self. If you embrace the power the Lord holds, you will enhance your time slot in that your motive for knowing gain and incentive will be grafted to a solid form of enhanced understanding. God does not accept a divided bond. You must admonish His goal for a joined interconnected union without holding on to a former love such as material gain. Working for a living is right and true but focusing on cash as a god is false in that it will not testify on your behalf come judgment hour. You alone can choose whether you may gain entry to heaven's gate. The responsibility is yours. God does not lead anyone into a blank unity of a false endeavor of no grounding. God's way is secure and forthright. He will provide the needed ministry for each witness to be heard. If you follow a pattern of listening to Him speak, you will proceed in a clear and precise action of forward gain, without the lie of power as your inheritance. God is the one in control. He serves man, but He is not beneath him. No one is ever secure if they pursue a kingdom's riches but lose the Father's arm upon their person.

Would you offer another a way to inherit riches if it would cause them to lose their life? God makes it clear that all who follow His lead will be protected and cared for without worrying about where their offerings will be found. God is the supplier of all things good. He can bring you a set standard or make you wealthy. By His choosing alone, we are granted material, monetary enhancement. If you stumble and fall, gain your footing by offering your repentance to the King. He will hear your request and remove the stain of sin where you will be tied to His directive once again.

God the Father and Jesus, His Son, are real and true. Neither branches against the other nor leads with deceptive maneuvers. With God, all things are right. There is never a loss incurred or a plan of deceit. God creates beauty in the style He produces. He is a crafter and a Waymaker. He does not harvest false pretenses or incur a body of lies. When one applies the Word of God in his make-up, he never loses his way. His steps will be planted in a gracious manner, and there will be insight given. The caretaker God is a gift to mankind in the form of leadership, and true companionship embraces that balance, the love found only by listening to the connection you receive if you follow faithfully in His footsteps.

God has offered His Son as a sacrifice forever. In this process, He made the gift a living offering where all unity is grafted for eternal time. You can't wage war if you don't know the enemy. God procures for man the opportune element where grace is sufficient for all he does. A shower of hope is ever present if you embellish on His character and trust God to lead. When care is offered through love and faith, God receives it and grows the countenance. The seaward-bound ship never steers wrong when the wind is blowing it to the place of destiny. God alone is the actor where love and faith meet. It is the place where He is present and where He enjoys relating to His people. If you seek true commitment and hope, trust the Father to grant these gifts. He does not come against a person, nor does He entertain falsehood so that you can relate to Him with a clear conscience and a drive for better relational skills. God leads with precision and character. He is solid in how He portrays His heart, and you never have to wonder where He will place your thoughts or actions. It will be measured precisely to lift the spirit and not tear it down.

God will build in a manner befitting His person, so know that when you engage with His presence, you are offering Him your bounty of faith. Your faith will create unity, and you will learn how to speak and show a strong witness. God never leaves the heart in a tangle or with a detrimental persona. If you are in an entrapment, trust God to release you from it. Offer to Him the viable measure of a step forward in His direction. From there, you will gain more ground by accepting the way of His Lordship. You can learn all there is to understand if you trust what God gave to all, His love and Word to live by. He is a crafter and a way to be that reflects goodness and mercy. With God, one is ever present with good character, so he may always have a grace that enables him to seek kind measure and a truth, forward inclination.

Today the hope of man is not understood by those who follow in the way of deception. Many think they can serve themselves instead of Jesus. If you tend to think about how to improve your mindset, but you skip the study of God's Word, you are simply negating the true witness and power that awaits your instruction. God is at work in the manner of always moving in the direction of faith. You need to practice the measure of faith for this to occur. When a partner in line with your mental grasp comes forward and desires you to partake in his plan, are you not interested by way of opportunity? When God draws someone to His person, a light of eternal magnitude unfolds even though no real bounty is witnessed first-hand. A rest will occur within the mindset, and you will comprehend you have gained a mature undertaking where faith is present, and hope is justified. God will honor a work and bring a moral standard where He alone is the one to pour out good measure. If you gain rewards and find no joy, your heart is not connected to the call you are following. When God brings into play a witness, there resides a clear opportune enjoyment, and an offering of love is bestowed in the manner of true gain. God is not the giver of doubt or deceit. He will organize a plan and grow it in a forthright way of being. With His hand upon your direct witness, you will offer to another hope and a mental, true conduit of a structure with a pure thought process. You won't simply invest in yourself. You will desire many to learn the good news you have witnessed. God plans the upright and forward motion of delight. His caretaking is solid, and it grafts to the spirit a gallant mannerism where faith is produced in relation to growth. If you try to gain monetary wisdom but not spiritual enhancement, you will find a loss of purity and fall victim to the desire for riches alone. All of man desires to be well fed. The nature of God is to feed and to grant favor when trust is applied in His direct correlation to whoever is advancing their mindset toward His person. Look at how the Lord has favored the group of people named His special body of believers, the Israelites. He never pursued a weaker group in all of history. They represent man and his weak behavior. We all choose poorly at times. We all make mistakes, and we stumble and lose our way, but because of the cross, we are washed clean and made redeemable in love and faithfulness.

> *Do not forget the covenant I have made with you, and do not worship other gods. Rather, worship the Lord your God; it is he who will deliver you from the hand of all your enemies." 2Kings 17:38-39 NIV*

With man's focus on himself, there is little faith being expressed. It is the height of man in his mental anguish. Serving in the way of God brings hope in which all who tell of His honor are subject to a life of great rewards. God knows man and how he operates. He is the designer and creator, yet He is separate in how He proceeds with each one. Many assume a life committed to God offers little in the way of excitement or joy. This is false and reflects a lie. God knows the spirit and how to uphold the mind, so it relishes in the work or play God crafts. God leads man in a clear way, and He grants favor when there is a solid mental ordained lead in which hope is mastered and understood. Looking at faith as a drawback is false with a pretense that there is no real lead or host of good measure. God is the source of all dreams. He is the builder of the mind, and He brings to the table a plan to make a solid investment grow. If money is not present, you may need to entertain the reality that what you desire is not the plan God has for you. If you have seen much development, then a sudden stop in production, there may be a reason God hasn't moved. You may be gaining insight in the form of knowledge or even a spiritual gain of power in the form of belief. It may be on the horizon, just not visible in its current state. God offers all the opportunity to know Him personally, so when you speak to His person, remember He knows what you have to say before you say it. There is no delivery he hasn't thought of or known; even your tears speak to His heart. If words fail you, let your spirit be led by His power and pray with the hope He will advance your cause and move it to a manageable fracture. God is careful in His placement of trust. A weak person will not inherit a profound body of build. It won't balance if he is tried. The ground won't support a weak frame; just as a structure needs a solid foundation, so does the operator need a true course. God builds and releases the opportunity when the time is conducive to His mindset. It can take days, or the trial period can be months, even years. All things work for good for those that love the Lord.

Look at how God has implemented the art of knowledge to those who trust His person. Many have learned how to proceed with a craft even before they entered the management element of their study. When presented with care, a learned manner will greatly enhance your performance, where your work and attitude reflect a current mindset that all you endeavor to do is for the glory of the Master, whom we call Lord. The fact that no one else ever created the world states we are not as gifted as God Himself. No one can compare to the power God holds. He is an element of great fortitude and a manner of faith when it comes to real commitment. God always operates in the realm of truth. He is not able to lie or cheat. He never invests in the weak to cause them harm. He supports their work when it is true and just and plans for them to gain in the way of good measure. Even if it appears none is on the table, God will bring about a setting where all comes to a point of good enlightenment. The caretaker you need is Christ. He alone is the Waymaker. He never fails and is always the one seeing to the goal of goodness. With God, you can retrieve a soft landing and dine on intellect where all is measured and found wholesome.

The feature of a cold detail where you have not understood how to proceed may be a saving grace. God may have a purpose in the way of a silent understanding that He is at work paving the way. One may follow the thought that there is another need being ministered to in which the timetable will reflect the pause. Seeing where to plant is important. In the rear-view mirror, one knows how they should have performed. If you have not been given a clear thought on how to go about the necessary measure, you need to trust the Lord to bring clarity. Waiting is often a difficult feat. The mind wants to harbor the truth and relishes in the growth process. However, waiting may bring into play the necessary means you have been waiting upon. Your goal may fit the product line, but God's action is what gets the whole balance underway. Trust His leadership and know He is always at your side.

The Lord is a Waymaker. He never instructs without a purpose or a plan of unity. With Him, you can become a solid presentation of good character in the form of growth with a perspective that God alone is the Master behind your success. Look at how He encapsulates the mind and sheds light on the region of truth. You never have to wonder where you can find love or hope as He is always willing to shower you with these qualities and shade your heart in a pure design connected to His personality type. The Lord is always benefiting a guide with care and honest, moral, heart-shaped monologs of trust. Leveraging the mind in the hope of a solid build can only be accomplished when faith is at the forefront in all you seek. Look to the Father and see His good line and form. It is found on the pages of every Bible where He has planted His thoughts and actions so that we may know Him better. Reading gives the mind clarity. It does not offer the written hope of wealth but of knowledge where great understanding resides. A path of righteousness is what God looks for. He leaves our decision-making to our own insight, but He puts forth the related guide and delivers us into knowledge when we embrace His instruction and believe He will act on our behalf. God is not here to judge and leave us alone to fend off the enemy on our own. He makes our needed environmental integrity clear, and He offers to our hearts the message of true merit where we follow His lead and grow in strength. God is a unity maker. He is the one to form a true course and a steadfast level of enticed knowledge that operates as a lead in our favor. It is our own decision to follow and heed His purpose in our lives. What we see as good for our way of life is determined by whether we want God as our lead or our mental understanding of His might and power. We can't compare to His greatness, so our understanding of things is quite small in relation to Him. If you think you know more than the maker of mankind, you will escape the great truth and be led into hardship, be it in the form of decay from a disease or perhaps a loss in financial standing. Your situation may require an act of God to make you more pliable to His call. Learn the Word and see how you can restore your ground and be set free in the way of understanding. Blindness is easily placed on a heart when God is removed from the onslaught of sight. With

Him, there is real truth and hope. Without God, you find grace is a vapor. It only permeates the spirit when God is in control. If you surrender to the Most High, you receive a way forward without guilt and shame. Your heart is restored, and a fine, mental development of good truth enters. You will learn faith plays a role in the process. It is what anchors the spirit to God and draws Him near. If you find favor, you will realize God's way is always the best, which will bring the spirit of joy. Recognizing God's love is something we don't invest in enough. Reflect on what God has done for you and how He has taken you under His wing. You may feel you were the one to gain but know God is the one who performs the goals and offers the dream. Without Him, no good thing materializes.

With the market of hope as God's incentive, we never have to wonder where His heart rests. We are shown His good nature in the words of David found in scripture.

> *But I trust in your unfailing love; my heart rejoices in your salvation. I will sing to the Lord, for he has been good to me. Psalm 13;5-6 NIV*

Assimilate Christ's character into your heart and mindset. He will instruct you in the way you should go. A bounty will be had when you realize God is the one to offer the hope you need to proceed in any embankment of ground where you wish to succeed. God is willing to offer His steps to bring into play a sound, opportune management style that brings the light of day into the night. His character is solid, so worry has no place. He can bring delight with a motive of true gain or even insight that expands in the form of grand endeavors. God does not harden a situation. He enables it to move forward with care and love as its focus. If you have an abundance of moral righteousness, you are gifted because God favored your vision. If you apply this gift and build in strength, you reveal a moral knowledge that you alone are not enough. People who trust God's leadership find a rich and fruitful path. It may be difficult or labor-some, but the reward will be recognized as God's hand alone. God is the crafter of hearts, and He knows who features a care for His person. He has embellished the mind of all with His love, but not all choose to know Him personally. Whom we follow is reflective of who we choose in life as our Lord. You may not think you have chosen a god, but the spirit is inclined to pursue one of a higher being. It is in our design and makeup. Trust the Word of the Lord. He has offered our hearts a way to know Him and to embrace His person. No other god offers a connection in which one can be grafted to the King of all and know Him personally. It is a measure easily accomplished if you recognize you need to know Jesus as Lord. The words of any prayer confessing unrighteous behavior and a need for redemption are all that is required. In the profession will reside the needed mechanism of faith so God can act and deliver a redeeming spirit from His Son to you personally. Trust the act to be complete once the words are recited from your heart to His. This is where you connect as one and a bond is formed.

God is the one who offers a parallel founding for all who trust His leadership. An offering of love is found on every page of written material the Bible outlines. You won't find a better caretaker. He alone is the Master of this greatness. God works to inhibit raw thoughts that lead to unplanned misfortune. He will never leave the basis of true character or doubt. He is always faithful and pursues the mind in love, not hostility. With God, you are able to build with a free gift in which the mind is received as a unity in faith and good, moral, uplifting bylaws. The shoulder of the Lord is broad. You need not fear His ability to grant an honorable stand in the way you focus or pursue Him. If a thought of immoral lead enters the scene know it is not the Savior at work but a false lead of sin and corrupt, mental gain. Gaining in the way of ill-gotten measure brings a dark hold that causes one to lose focus on who the character of God is. He will never allow one to build in His name if false pretense is the goal. He will tear down the legacy in one form or another. Looking for the incentive is a process one learns to develop over time. Reading and having a prayer life in the Word supplies the mind with an accurate balance and a hope for tomorrow. Without this incentive, there can be no unity of what God holds true to be a bond and unity where He can work. Many believe they can skip measures when they build, only to find a wreck on their hands with no solid footing to balance it again. A plan of integrity must have at its core the love of who the Lord is and who He represents.

You can lead many into false persuasion, but at some point, the wall of injustice will collapse, and all will be for naught. If you desire a solid base with true, moral, reflective guidance, offer your time and heart to the Lord. He will then build a formal ground in which you desire to know Him more and He will be your focus. Reading the Word allows His presence to draw near, and it grants the privilege of knowing Him in a personal manner. Grace covers the rest, and you will know a wave of peace in which your heart rejoices and captures the love of many.

Message Four

Care is God's Support Structure

The favor of God is not always a bank account of great wealth or a home of significance, but it can be a moral richness where faith is secure and love is abundant. If you follow the Savior, you will learn a pattern of hope in which your heart and body will follow suit, and you will be gifted a unique guideline for all your endeavors. The truth you will adhere to will be personal, and you will gain an interest in the plan the Lord has for you. You won't wonder whether to act or stay put if a clear understanding is presented because you will have mastered the connected, good measure of faith and have a design of truth before your heart. God offers every person the gain of intellect when they pursue Him personally. If you trail behind in the way of confidence, know God can build within you a learned, mental gain that you are His child, which measures the mind at a true juncture where peace of true kinship is known. You will gain confidence, and inspiration will follow. You won't be afraid to trust when it comes time to step forward into the work of progressive, forward lineage.

The comfort of the home is often a barrier to more intellect as a person realizes he forgets to gain knowledge when he rests. If you look into what the Bible has to say about the strength you will learn when reading the contents, it will offer a bond and unity where your aptitude for more knowledge begins to grow. It is a pleasure to learn true meaning and to gain intellect where knowledge is peace and hope. The beginning may seem tedious as the process is a new behavior, but soon the bounds of inhibition will fade, and your desire will be kindled, and you will pursue the one called Jesus with a fever. This is the connected unity that transpires. You will also gain insight and be blessed with an understanding of how to act your faith. Reading passages balances the mind and offers the heart a compatible love it desires to know. God has placed in all of man the desire to know Him personally. Because of grace and the death and resurrection of Jesus, we can have this unity. The power of this act offers a path where all of man can be saved whether you accept the pull you feel within or reject it is your choice alone. God won't force His way into your presence. He is gentle and full of compassion. He never forces His will onto your mindset. That is not His way. He is a caretaker and a lover of the soul. God grants favor through the message of His spirit. It is up to us to accept the gift and pursue Him as our first love. Without this action, there is no real bond and no hope for instruction in the nature of real gain.

You may accept the Savior but never really learn who He is. Your witness will not thrive, and you won't hold the heart in esteem. You will walk in a cloud without truth and venture into plans and schemes without the protection of the spirit. When you apply your thought process to the King, great things form around your heart. You learn how to balance the world and how to invest in wise indulgences without losing your solid footing. God will honor a person who pursues Him with faith. One who steps in accordance with the fact God is the way gains the true understanding that hope resides with God alone.

People often wonder where God is in times of trouble. Is He there when a person dies? Is He ever present as His Word describes? God alone can meet all the material strength required to gain hope and fortitude where man can assimilate the care and desire of a witness of good measure. Only God can bring about a plan that enables a forward motion to obtain a mighty way of thinking. With God, we operate in a manner of goodwill and strength. God has allowed our hearts to embrace one another. He has designed our spirit to balance the need for personal ties with someone other than ourselves. Even though many find solitude tranquil and majestic, we are, by our makeup, joined to one another spiritually.

People often wonder where God is when a disaster strikes. He is present then as well. He cares for the sick and the hurt in a manner that only He can provide. He offers to those in pain the benefit of His healing and His thought of control when losing a perspective that God is real. He never brings to earth a plan of hardened abandonment. He is always caring and solid with love at His core. His grace is sufficient in times of trouble in that you will know He is at work, making a path that leads to better days. Your outlook will determine whether your spirit is united to His in the manner of faith and hope. God is not limited to the study of life and its goals. He knows all and sees all. He doesn't step away when hard times strike. This is simply due to the fall of man. God did not design our lives to be hard. He desired for all man to have much in the way of joy and kinship with His person. Because we have sin nature, our desire will be to come against God on occasion. This separates our witness, leading to a loss of connection otherwise enhanced by prayer and reading God's Word. If you look to advance your spirit dine on the fact God is sacred. He is not a deficit or detrimental to us in any form. When you expect God to move a certain way, you lose the understanding that God is superior in all He does. His plan is always the best. We may desire our own advancement, leading us to believe we should have our own way. God knows the proper way, and He will apply this standard to the way of life He desires for you to learn through. His care is sufficient and wholesome. With God, our plan will fade, and His will be embellished upon. God is great, and He manages the mind with great care, always making a desire His own. He does not forget that man needs instruction. This He offers freely, so enter into prayer and be lifted up into the realm of pure knowledge. With God, we entertain the right outlook, and a perspective of faithfulness ensues.

God is the one to offer hope mixed with pleasure. He grafts the heart with a motive that brings into play the design is where a plan of true worth is brought forward. God organizes the mind and incorporates the heart to succeed in a formal and true gateway leading to a forest of intent that is good in all it represents. Staking a claim to the heart of man is the symbol God shared when His Son hung from the tree of crucifixion. God ordained man to be a character in grace that limits the perception God alone is the Master plan. His desire is for man to know Him personally and to meet Him in the pages of His Book. The Bible offers all that is needed to faithfully follow the Lord's way. Through reading, you gain insight and the hope of a future where you may reside with God above. Jesus is the connection we lean into for this to happen. Because of God's commitment, we never have to fear that we will fall away. Salvation is for all time. The profession of faith carries with it the stamina and retention that God is always with you forever. You can lean into this truth and reveal its properties, simply offer your heart and mind into God's control. He won't override your thought process. He will give you clarity with a connected bond in where you learn who the Father is and how to know Him personally. Each person who has accepted that Jesus is real and claimed Him as their Savior dines on the connected bond they have gained. A light reading of the Word of God draws Him into your presence, and you gravitate closer to His person. A day of witness can produce much favor when it is guided by the hand of God. Your shadow is not measured by how you stand. It is a distorted underlying shape. When God applies understanding, you gain in the form of unity with His person. You will harvest the knowledge that you are His partner, but He is the lead and head of the team. All you have accomplished is measured by whether your care was genuine or you were doing it for self-gain. Supporting another is a gift in its own right. Offering your talents to aid someone to complete their own goal is held in high esteem. In the view of God, it is righteous and pure.

The love found in scripture is solid in the form it presents. The power you gain is pure and free from doubt. With God, the moral grace you receive is ever present, and you gain a character where faith is at your back door. Allowing the Father to move within your spirit brings you to His center, and there you find hope. His character is pure, so you know you will learn with care, and a direct motive of trust will guide your thought process. The light of God is offered to any man who trusts He is who He claims to be. If you doubt but desire to know the truth of who God is personally, you must first request Him to enter your spirit. You must be willing to learn in the form of an engaged body between you and Him.

Without this commitment from you personally, a unified balance won't transpire. You must be willing to accept God is in control and that you on your own cannot bring relief to your weary soul. God is the only one to enhance the mind along with the heart. He delivers the unified perception required for one to know Him personally. Jesus is the bridge that brings this to admittance. Without Christ, one will never know who God the Father is or His subsequent gift of salvation. God honors any attempt toward Him personally. If you are weak, ask His help to be laid within your mind and heart. He will offer you this reprieve, and you will then be able to hear His draw to you. Without the power of God, we all would be lost. Some gain truth easier than others. This is not because one is greater or less. It is due to a willing spirit. If you desire to hold on to your mental guidance, it will be difficult for you to embrace another in the form of faith.

God invests in all who accept His invitation. He freely embraces a child and leads them to the throne of justice. No one can be led without the knowledge that they are not the one with the power. God is the achiever. He alone separates the goats from the sheep, meaning He knows who is faithful and who pretends. If you accept you are a sinner with a sinful nature, you realize you need redemption. This is the act Christ died for. The cross was a balance beam, and it offered to man the needed maintenance stream that gifts the mind and body with a pure dose of tangled love.

You can find a gateway at the bottom of a bottle, but it will lead to death. Many serve the master of darkness when they think they have the cure themselves. If a spirit of unity is drawing, you question who it comes from. Is salvation offered, or does the flavor of riches or drugs entice you? Are you centered in the thought process, or do you recognize there is one greater? Are you offered peace, or is there a pull for more greatness outside of one who is pure? Is your heart encapsulated with love, or are you seeking a fast track to greatness? Where your heart lies, there will be your true acceptance of what is good. God offers a land of milk and honey in the form of a true recognized landing. The pad is relinquished but ever great in its ability to withstand trials and heartbreak. When you accept God, you learn a true, righteous, developmental way of being. You aren't lost but found, natural and holy.

Looking at the Savior as simply a pal is inaccurate in its display. God is superior. It is true He is close and offers us companionship, but His person needs to be seen as great and not equal to our level of achievement. If you believe God is equal, you lose the personal gift that He is the Master. God is not shallow or misrepresented by His character. He is pure, and the balance He holds is always right. We cannot offer to be such a creation, for we are weak in our desires. God puts forth beauty where He is great but not haughty. God is our Father. He rules over us as a leader, strong and prosperous in the way he moves. Sometimes we lose our footing and fall, whether intentional or because we don't trust in the way God offers us to be stationed in our path. When a person loses the perspective that God will provide, he then concentrates on how to bring prosperity to his gain. This deception leads to a loss of integral bounty, and no real hope is projected. Losing a partner brings with it a hard measure of faith. Will you need something outside of the Savior, or will you understand that God gifts to those who pursue Him and believe He will give bounty in the form that is needed? Wealth is not the measure of how God feels toward His people. Many learn real happiness is granted in the giving process.

God's favor is pure. When He bestows a gift, it is freely given. He won't demand a prejudice against you. Those who give but expect a return are not offering a spirit of love but of loan management. If your heart desires to offer others more in the way of mutual funds, know God has moved within you. He is the granter of all things right and true. When God speaks, our hearts embrace the lead and act accordingly. Whether it be to offer a new line of integral sacrifice or to balance a budget. All measure of unity is found by the hand of God. He brings to the table a clear help, and with it is a note of purity. God is honest with no guilt preceding any opportune embellishment. The truth of who God is may not be favorable to some. Those are the ones who never trust or believe another would be right and true. Man has caused many heartaches, but the favor of the Lord is ever pleasant. The heart accepts the purity of God; whether the mind delivers this gift is solely up to the individual. Each of us must determine who to follow. It is written upon the heart of man to search and learn who is King. When you meet Him, you dine on the discovery. Even those who reject God learn in the end that their path was forsaken, but it is too late, and the door has closed.

Message Five

God is Personal to All People

The look of unity God has portrayed in the Word offers us to know gains in the manner of great love. God works in favor of a gift for man to know Him, and to learn His faith is occupational. God is the host where faith resides. Each doorway is bright when God the Father relays His true character and presents a pathway where man can gain knowledge where he never loses solid guidance. A love so grand is what God portrays with each detail presented in the unity of prayer and the reading of the Bible. Trust God to work in a manner that is right and true. He won't calculate a loss or bring pain. That is not His way. God offers the mind gentle guidance in where you learn how to step and where to go forward. God does not harden a man against Him. If this is the case, the one who rejected God is liable in that he never followed suit in favor of love and trust. With God, we must believe He will provide, and we blindly follow His lead and direct course of measure. God will not harbor a man against his brother. He will not ask one to follow a dark path or one of misfortune. God designs man to be a spirit of good and hope. When a walk has been granted, God can bring aboard a pattern of intent where all parties gain intellect and a clear viewpoint. Leading one to allow more growth is an example in which the Lord reveals the plan of salvation through another's actions. If you look to the left or the right and lose the perspective God is straight ahead, you will lose focus and fall into a pit. A snare will be set, and you will need intervention to come into the light once again. Read the Word of God and stay on the course of enlightenment. Without it, you will guarantee a loss comes your way. Taking the Word of God at face value brings the understanding that God is the Master. He is the way forward, and He can supply all your needs. With this in mind factor in His capable way of being and you will believe the reality God can do no harm. God will supply you with hope when needed, and He will guide you with a clear mental enlightenment to offer a plan where you know how to step. God is at work at all times, making a sure amount of faith is available. Enter into His presence and be assured you know the formula to gain in the manner of integral mannerisms. The Savior is rich with love. Embrace His character and be enlightened. He holds your heart, and He never leads it astray. You can know Him personally and lean into Him in times of trouble. Call on His name, and you will have a partner for life who is faithful and right with a bounty of opportunistic motives.

When God moves, His spirit is bound in the unity it offers to our heart. He cares about every detail we have aspired to, and He prepares an opportune moment for goodness to emerge. Allowing God the freedom to move within our nest of character brings a mature hope that He will provide. If you find a slow pace has ensued, rest in the knowledge God brings to the table a guide where His favor is abundant. God does not allow deception to emerge without giving light to the situation in golden moments of clarity. You may have thought you understood the will of God only to find you were led astray by your delighted thought process. God will deliver the truth, and you will understand grace has been at work rebuilding your heart's desire. The plan you have harbored may be replaced by a new formula and pattern in which you feel complete and at peace. If you still hope for the same entity to come to pass, rely on the thought God may be building for you, a direct vision where hope is at the core. God offers His insight when the heart is ready to receive God's plan. You may not realize the mercy God prepared, but when the final verdict is determined, you will come to know God was ever faithful and right in His decision. Walking in the light is the pattern of right thinking. With it comes the subject of great honor. You can't walk blindly yet expect God to deliver a plan without the gain of knowledge coming into plain sight. If you offer to God your dream and wait for Him to show you the lead, you will have benefited in the way you should go. With God, all things work to good even when the understanding is different than you had planned. God knows best and puts forth the energy to correct a misdirect where a false representation has been administered. Look at what is in front of your thought process. Is there an option where you can make a difference yet stay true to your desire? Is there a path where you can build opportune methods of hope yet not be enslaved to the spectrum of the commitment? Can you proceed through in a manner not centered around the focus of your delight? Can you wage a direct course of action not detrimental to the bounty you hold? Has there been an open door, just not the vision for how to make it come into play? The consideration of strength is an object one can adhere to as well. God is all-powerful. He can build in the form of unity in which you understand what is to follow and how to pursue a plan that doesn't bring harm or despair to the work you have crafted. He will lead and build for you a way, and you will recognize His soulful admonishment to your thought process. God cares about you, and He will not bring a work that you have little help in obtaining. He will deliver to your spirit a bounty where knowledge is graced with ability. Trust His guide and let Him care for you as a Father would. Know Him as a rewarder of grace and faith.

God's character is a gift to all men. In the process of study, the learning curve gains ground with each word taken into account and underlined with clear mental focus. If you feel cheated by another, look at whom you serve. God the Father offered to man His Son the Holy Grail and caretaker of mankind, yet many do not believe. This process of doubt comes against the person of God daily. Day and night, He endures rejection and heartache. Man, though weak, still seeks to be his own manager. He falls short but turns his back on the light and reseeds into the dark. How God endures disgrace is with character and a solid formula of strength. He is not weak nor is He shallow. His person is great with a lead of mental rebound none can compare. God does not harbor a grudge nor step away when He is offended. He endures the wait and knows man is His child who needs a Savior. Christ is the solitude man finds when he accepts the gift of unity found at the cross. You can always guess how to know which plan is yours or which desire is from God, but when you follow what is written, you will obtain a connected, real understanding of where you fit in the world of man. Are you a follower, or do you want to lead? Do you embrace God as head, or are you unwilling to serve Him financially or respectfully? We must surrender all to Him if we wish to have Him as our God. God will not steal what you own. He may direct you to release goods that hold you bound, but it will better your standing and graft you closer to the King. Only a false god brings with it success of pride. If you find joy in all you have created but don't give God the glory, you are making it an idol. God is the one who gave you the dream and the entitlement in which you were able to craft and make your desire come true. If you recognize this as fact, you have gained insight into the nature of the Most High. God allows us to have personal gains, but He places within us the knowledge that is the reason we have them. Allow the purpose God has presented to be your focus. Watch Him move as a result and follow the lead He offers. You will nurture the desire He puts forth when you apply your time to His Word and prayer is placed at the helm of your day. With God, clarity is revealed, and true knowledge of His desire springs forth. Trust Him and be at peace in the direction He takes you. Accepting the meaning of faith is to connect your spirit to the King bringing the needed bond to formulate a true wealth wherein all you accept from the Savior is right and true.

God is the resource for man to invest in. With Him as your anchor, the tide will wash but never unseat your will and desire to grow in a good and prosperous manner. God holds the key to a better life. In Him, you will learn a true way of developing a common approach to build a lasting encounter and framework of good study. Teaching may affect your spirit, and you will desire to tell others about the Savior and His good character. Leaning into the Word will aid your outreach and better equip your routine to enhance your ability to instruct and carry forward the witness knowing where to place your trust. God alone is the way, and He is the solid material goal to strive for. All other ways outside of Christ are dark and deceptive. They are not secure, nor will they bring you a solid way of homecare. God does not leave you to pursue another. He is always standing ready and in place with a maneuverable means of gaining intellect that surpasses the onslaught of dark dreams. God will procure a standard where your heart hears a good plan and knows where the faith needs to be placed. Chasing the money trail will bring rewards, but they are not the kind in which the spirit is balanced and secure. A bank account can hold much in the way of a future debt in that it only erases a bill. It cannot hold a heart and restore the mind. If you have sought to gain wealth all the while kneeling on the bed of hope that God will enable you to accumulate vast wealth, you have lost the focus of what is important. He may offer you time in where you live longer because your wealth enabled a healthy lifestyle, but where will you rest on judgment day? Have you poured into others in the form of true invested goods and services? Has your heart hoped for others to know Jesus and meet Him personally for themselves as Lord of their whole being? Are you one who dines on the truth and enlists God's principles so that others are led to the same cause you stand for? Where will your glory be if you have forgotten the reason for true righteousness? It will fade with death, and only a small remembrance shall exist. If you have taken it upon yourself to invest in others and to shield their mind with the knowledge that God is all-powerful, you have done well. Looking to gain solely for your bank account does not bring hope or prosperity where your heart rests in peace.

Taking from others by way of influence is not a support God envisions as good either. Be true to what God expresses in His Word. Look at how you can bring others hope and fruitful gains. With God, all works of true balance and good measure reflect who the Father is and how He relates to His people. Stepping toward the light will involve a sweet gathering between you and Jesus. He will connect with you when a prayer is recited and offered in true faith. Outside of God, all fail because there is no hope for redemption. Knowing your commitment to Christ is what makes the difference. You can't escape from the true knowledge presented in the Word. You can deny or reject it, but it stands as whole and righteous with legs of truth.

Reading scripture is a mechanism by which man can build for solid growth where God can relate and offer hope to the mind. When you feel lost or without importance, look at how God speaks of those, He built bonds within His material of the Bible.

> *The Lord has said to Abram, "Leave your country, your people and your father's household and go to the land I will show you. I will make you into a great nation and I will bless you; I will make your name great, and you will be a blessing. I will bless those who bless you, and whoever curses you I will curse; and all peoples on earth will be blessed through you. Genesis 12:1-3 NIV*

The teaching of the Lord enhances the mind and delivers the true way of being. With this process, man can communicate and learn where to look for faith and how to present the mind into a state of acceptance toward the King. Christ is the reason for our salvation. He is the Waymaker. Through His death, all of man gained the opportunity to know Him personally and to reside with His person on any given day. Whether we are alive on this earth or have passed on to the sky above God will always welcome our advances toward Him. God is the caretaker of our hearts. He is the reason we all have hope or light within our spirit. Anyone searching for a better way need only invest in the partnership with the Almighty. He will advance and adhere to your quest and lead you toward the goal of righteous integrity where His person resides. Darkness has no divine mental outlook. It simply carries lies and deceptive thought processes that breed unholy mannerisms. Grab onto the fact God will offer faith, and with it will be His acceptance of your honor toward Him. Building a picture of unity is the process God will inflict when you accept Him as Lord and deliver your faith to Him personally. Your cry for Him to carry you over broken ground will erupt in a manner where your spirit dines on hope and grows in the deliverance of free, heart felt gifts of the spirit.

People of today represent a fallen world. Man thinks he alone can build and create without regard for the Master and His righteous accountability. Anyone who builds for himself alone does not truly understand the opportunity presented by the King. If you look at how He operated in scripture, you glean a knowledge that Christ is the Waymaker. He often opened doors and led people when they were suffering and lost in their sins. Each delicate maneuver was crafted with care, and as a result, many learned the favor of God was with them. The honor God hosts is talent and true, moral righteousness. No other has the gift of greatness that God alone contains within Himself. Our eyes and hearts see clouds in the sky, but man does not understand how they got there. God is the one who harvests and plants. He may have used the hands and feet of man to do so, but He is the one to build in the way of growth. No seed would sprout if God did not direct it to do so. He is the Waymaker. He crafts with care and supports plans that speak of light. If you dream of creating a mission where light is offered that follows the Gospel, you will be honored for your efforts. God will make a way for your plans to be fruitful, where hope will reside, and you will know goodwill.

God, the Father crafts in a manner that brings forth much that represents true character, and an offer of genuine insight is gleaned. Planning on the defense brings a tide of gentle, maneuverable aspects that glean a path toward the goal of real leadership. Balance will reside, and your heart will connect with a desire to gain more insight from the King. When Jesus speaks, your heart embraces the light and yearns for more knowledge. If you find a step where no growth transpires, wait and see what door is opened and what balance is offered where you can move in a lateral position, gaining more grace. A wait may simply mean growth needs to shape the mind and the heart. God works through His people. He offers a path with clear understanding and enhances the knowledge one needs to perform the goal at hand.

The stand offered by the hand of God will offer a form of unity in the way of grace. You will adhere to a plan in which your mind can comprehend the needed outline and how it will affect each requirement written in your heart. If a plan is formed, but no real integral unity is presented, you are being misled, and deceit is present. God operates in the manner of hope with purpose. Every step is clear and understood as good and hopeful. Your heart will desire the manner presented, and you will have peace. You will know God is the one who brought about the good measure, and your faith will be a shield as well. If clouds are cast, and you are experiencing a delay, trust the Lord is protecting you from destruction. It can be difficult and grueling when a dream is on hold, but the purpose for the wait may surprise you in the end. All the work of God is righteous. It never harbors a plan and then leaves it to rust. God works for the favor of His name. He supports the body and accepts His shortcomings. God is the great creator. He knows every detail that must transpire. With His care, all good things develop in the right time frame. Working toward a goal brings the desire for completion.

A pattern of pure glory will reveal the goodness God held while the wait was underway. Trust God to enlighten the mind when He deems fit. His timing never forgets the mind of His people. He knows their limits, and He reflects all good hopes. God can offer man a reprieve in which a new understudy may develop to fill the void in the recessed timetable. You will have a new inspiration to build within, and you can move forward with faith and a positive format while the grace is underway. You will be at peace, not letting go of what is to come but bending to the will of God and trusting He is at work, making a way for your dream to present as a whole. The timetable may adjust where both of the works you have invested in are joined, and they become a unified body. God knows how to prepare any uplift of the spirit. He knows how to craft and create, so no one suffers or loses faith. He will instruct the mind while faith resides and build character as a unified persona to His person. A witness of true, moral insight remembers God alone is the Master. With Him, the heart can find safety and know a bed of integral worship which meets the Creator in a unified center of faith. We, the people, are a reflection of who the Savior is; if faith has carried you to the gate of belief, risk the next step and walk through with Christ at your side.

Prayer is the mechanism that offers us free entry toward the King. God is the light we all hope to know. Your spirit will call to Him, and you will enhance the process when you read the Word of God. If you have doubt, look at how Simon Peter felt when he lost faith and rejected who Christ was out of fear.

Then Peter remembered the word Jesus had spoken: "Before the rooster crows, you will disown me three times." And he went outside and wept bitterly. Matthew 26:75 NIV

When Jesus offered Peter the knowledge that he would lose faith, Peter chose to think he would withstand the dark moment to come. However, the Word of God is always true. The fact Peter lost strength did not represent he had fallen out of love with God. It simply spoke to his weak person. All of man is weak when hardship presents in the form of danger. Trusting in God through the process is what makes one able to continue toward the fact of hope with a new measure of grace. An envelope of fear can bring into play doubt where one stumbles and loses their footing. God is ever-present. He can lead a lost person back to His saving grace with a simple spoken word as a reminder of who He is in that individual's life. God operates in a manner that is solid and just. People often relate to only the good He offers without knowing what harm may come their way in the form of an outside influence. Even though God is just, He allows a person to separate if they choose. A dark veil can ensue, and one may find it hard to acknowledge their sin. When God recedes, the layer that formed on the eyes, wisdom enters the mind, and a newfound strength ensues. A shadow is cast on the darkness, and it is swept away. If someone feels alone, the Word of God can bring light to their soul. A new form of commitment can induce a plan in which strength is abundant, which in turn brings clarity. Guarding the heart is wise. You can't expect knowledge to flow into your person when you don't feed it the Word of God. God is the creator of all good things. His Word is developed so man may have the needed tool to always stay in a committed correspondence with the Almighty, where he will grow with intellect and not be deceived. The power of God's Word grafts to our spirit knowledge and we see with eyes that are enhanced in the manner of a secure witness from God Himself. Your Father is ever safe and abundant in His caregiving. A mighty wind will blow through His grace, and you will have protection within your spirit. Trust is what enhances God to you personally. This is where your own mental gain completes the process of love from God to you alone.

Teaching others to know who the Lord and Creator are is a gift of love that offers the sound judgment that God is superior to all of man. If you pursue the faith burden, you can overcome the dark thoughts that press into your mind. God is always light. He does not offer sin as a solution. He does not hinder the mind with a dark presence, nor will He ask you to step forward and steal from another. If you have taken something that belongs to another, you should release the bounty and offer it back with a heart of repentance. Skilled people understand how to interact with someone who steps in the circle of faith they follow. If you teach others to gain through faith, you have gifted them with special knowledge of how to honor God. Not all realize their walk represents what their character says about them. If you have fallen, place your feet at the throne of God and embrace His person. Seek redemption and be delivered. God can use your witness and build a resume in which your fall from grace can be seen as a time of reflective opportunity. You can instruct another as to the proper path to follow. We all have had embarrassing failures in which we wish we had stepped faithfully, but these times can bring truth to others in the manner of distinct, orchestrated measures of integral faith. If you pursue God and pray for more deliverance, you will understand that you are a child of God. In this knowledge is the bounty that your harvest may gain hope and offer a clear, mental display of where to walk and how to balance your faith. Trust is what is a measure of your sure-footedness. When difficult times come across the heart, how you stand in the turmoil is what says who you believe you are. When you pursue the honor and hope God offers, you inherit the gift that you have value, and you are precious to God above. The plan God has in store is real, and it is beautiful. With Him, you gain a real motive for moving toward His person. Without the knowledge that you rest as a child in the arms of the great I Am, you will surrender in fear and fall prey to deceptive manners that will enlarge their course of action against you. Trust the Savior and build a connection that supports your mind and clears the confusion. You can gain a momentum of true honor and learn there is none more viable than the King Jesus. He is the Waymaker, and He brings to the table an honorable way of life in which you prosper and hold true to His kinship.

The heart of man is simple and in need of another to offer grace that binds and secures the mind and soul. God is ever-present, and He crafts with care. He is united to your person, and He delivers to your heart a hope that you will reside in the care and personage of the true King. God alone is the reason we all know one another in a spiritual connection. Our time together presents a unified bond, and we gain hope through a material witness that we are cared for. God is the Master at love. Through Him, we are granted the revelation our mind is inadequate in its ability to garnish others with influence unless we have been faithful to them as wise counsel. Someone may hover over you and truly not care, but in the long run, you will understand their true motive and lose faith. You will step away and be delivered from the negative influence they once held in your mind. It may happen suddenly or over time, but the grace of God will set you free. Looking toward the goal of faith, one recognizes there is none more valuable to pursue than the King of all, Jesus Himself. Anyone thinking they need someone outside of God has a blind commitment to His greatness. Understanding God will carry you over broken ground is a gift one acknowledges from unified trust. Walking on the coals of sand may not burn the skin, but the sharp fragments underfoot will cut and cause a wound.

In the same manner, a wound to the soul brings into play the thought of how to gain repair quickly. You will fall and lose your way if you step to the right or left. Your spirit must stand against the dark temptation to pursue an easy gain. Someone who hopes to cause you more discomfort along the path of righteousness may come. Not all who claim to accept you are being forthright. With a dark presence comes a lie, never a true goal of gain. Some hope to dissuade you from following the Lord. They will enact a plan to destroy your witness, which in turn leads many others out of the will of God.

Know that many watch and learn from your actions. A gracious hand may be presented with a stabbing knife in the other. True courtship will not ask you to go against your moral obligation to yourself or your King. When a lie is on the stage, look to where or from whom it was offered. Are they known to be righteous or honorable, or is their history one of deception? You may be a member of their household or even a distant connection to their life, but this will not hinder them from coming against you. God will reveal a motive if it is not of Him. He will secure your heart and speak words of life into your mind. A clear understanding will enter, and you will step away from the darkness. Many have fallen into the trap of adultery because another offered a ripe gift that was truly only a dark ploy to gain entrance to your thought process. If deception is on the table, know there is a way to resist. Look to scripture and gain freedom from the pull. Guard your heart and keep close to the knowledge that God is always on your team. He is the one who will give true meaning and offerings of unity without a purpose of discord. Gaining in the form of morsels from a lie is simply feeding one's own desire to no longer endure a pain. Give God the ailment. He has the salve and the bounty to repair any injury.

The manner of a man is to follow the easy path which leads to death. A witness where love is honored and scored as righteous comes from the Father. No other can bring into a body a hope or an elevated desire to gain more faith. God is the creator and the binder of the heart. If you desire to know Him personally, you have taken the thought of who He is and applied it to the understanding that He is who He says He is. With this in mind, belief is manifested by the work you ensue and follow. Your care toward the Creator is a benefit when it reflects His good name. If you allow God the ability to work in your life by accepting Him as your Lord, you open the stairway that leads to a glorious hope where you learn how to breathe in the truth. God supplies all men's needs through their work or a design of another form. God delivers the needed material for any form of hope in which a craft brings forth a display of created integral mindset and faith. The union God produces is a vision where all things good and right erupt into honor and hope. God alone is the Master who can cause a mind to balance an entire operating tool of love for another. When love is pure, there is no deceptive action within. A look at relationships that have stood the test of time reveals a commitment that has stabilized the transitional, gravitational pull of the heart. Any future hope of love after a failed marriage often brings a witness of lost faith. Many refuse to forgive and end in a disheveled form of dark regret. God has placed the mind to follow His lead. When a heartbreak ensues, love is what is sought after. Many fall prey to a lie just to be granted comfort for a time where they feel secure. But better is the way to stand and wait for God to reveal a path where your reflective mindset is adhered to Him alone. You may need to invest more time in the Word to better view how to compensate for the loss you feel. God heals the wound of love lost, and with it comes a hope that He alone will keep you secure. When this is understood, the knowledge is ever lasting. You will gain in the form of unity as well as the desire to be ever closer to the King. Don't replace the love of Christ with the love of man. You will only wallow in false praise, and self-denial will set in. The fact God alone is the mighty King should settle the thought that you need another, for no other can design a prayer or shelter a heart better than He. Prayer is what formulates the connected unity, and it restores the pipeline to His majestic overlay of desired intellect. In the process, you witness a true call to His person and reject the lie that another is needed. Love is not wrong when it is of character and skilled grooming. You can't bring a believer to a non-believer and hope for unity to blossom. One must be tied to Christ to have a relational bond in the form of devotion and care. Love is harvested when both partners trust the Lord for their direction and purpose in life. The unity is a blessed measure God offers to console our hearts and mind. It grafts us to a better mindset, so we stay connected. This process is what guides our hearts and minds and keeps us as one. Stepping away from God to please another is false misdirect. A lie has formed, and you fall daily until you realize that God is no longer first in your life. That is when you need the honor system of faith. Return to your first love and discover the reality of your situation. Seek forgiveness and plan to incorporate God as King in your daily walk. It may mean you have to separate and leave a relationship you have partaken in. But trust God to bring to you the needed desire to remain faithful. With this action, you are securing the position that God is the one you trust and serve. Balance your thought process with instructions from the

Bible and pray without ceasing. Your mind will clear, and you will learn once again how to proceed in faith. God is all willing to aid your steps through this process. Faith is subject to our heart and its ability to grow toward our Savior. Keep the Word of God as your focus, and be secure that God has a plan to better you. Time in the Word will build strength and character, resulting in favor, and God will enhance your walk with Him. This will bring the bounty your heart desires and restored unity will once again be front and center.

Message Six

God Recognizes Man as His Own

Man's desire is to grow and learn who God the Father and His Son are. In the learning of who makes the world and the sun, we gain the knowledge that there is a creator who is above all we know. Walking in faith brings to the heart the connected bond where God meets our mind and grants it the favor of unity with Him. The battle of knowledge between good and evil is won only when the enhanced patronage of reading the Word God transcribed for our gain is applied. If you grasp this understanding and relate it to all you do, your life will blossom, and knowledge will form that will be dressed in goodwill. God offers all this gift. He is not quiet when it comes to His commitment to our hearts. He speaks with a clear and calculated offering of love. He showers our hearts and minds with the knowledge that He will never leave our sides. He desires our goodwill to be applied so others too may know His person. The talent He gifts each individual is an onslaught in the form of gracious hope to better one another. If you reach toward the body of faith, you inherit much in the way of personal benefits. Each member holds a path of good measure that accumulates in measured integrity. If a fallen person reaches out to a trained counselor, they will learn a better way of life. If a false preacher offers a delight, but there is no real meat to his words, your spirit will acknowledge this offense, and you will dine on integrity in the place of deceit. A person with knowledge of how to inherit a vast amount of courage is valued for his strength. He may present as someone who is battle worn with frayed edges, but his bond with God will reflect a solid description of unity.

God cares for all who work to seek Him in a personal way. He will bestow to those the skillset to offer others the hope they have gained through personal ambition directed toward God. The flavor may host something you haven't personally tasted in the past, but its reflective nature will be that of purity. Walking on a path of righteousness comes with a calling card. You will know the voice of God when you hear it. If you are serving the community, your bounty will reflect a generous way with people. Your gift will be the ability to balance the love of God with a pattern of mature intellect in which you speak the truth of God to others through your care and honor for others' needs. Many acknowledge there is a God, but they don't invest in others around them. The voice you listen to may be of an ill, known manner that is not who God represents. His directive will be for others to gain through your experiences. Your truth and care are what will be seen, and they will draw the hearts of the hurting to you. This is what love entertains in the form of a good witness. Should you find time on your hands, think about how you can offer others care or words of encouragement. Is your daily commitment toward the goal of reflective desire, or do you think about who may need a helping hand? If you cannot serve physically, think about the gifts God has bestowed you that are not of the body. You can pray and offer wise counsel. You can question another's resources, or you can lift a spirit. The way you go about relating to others is what sets the bar as to who you desire to be like. Gossip brings pain in many forms. It can destroy a heart or break a will. Look to Christ for the measure of your thought process. A tiny display of faith brings forth the vision where your unity with God is visible. Offer hope and a glorified way of thought processes. Turn from hurtful manifestations of the mind and offer intellect with care. Make your word pure and justified. Refrain from leading others toward negative manners. Trust God to quiet your thought processes and bring them to a place of beauty.

Other's faults should be quieted and prayed for. It is better to remain silent than to overshadow the mind with dark enhances. Fill your day with sound attributes and speak joy to another's spirit. Pain breeds negative moral hygiene unless the Word of God is applied. Center your heart toward the will of God, and you will gain a perspective where your faith builds, and you will gain insight. Trust God to provide the needed historical witness and for Him to inject your comfort with care. He is all-powerful. He never fails. Your weakness is known to Him. All of man tires from the sin that surrounds him. A clear view will present itself with God, and your faith will grow. He offers to love and provide. Trust Him at His Word.

Faith is a subsequent way of gaining a design element that breaches the mind and offers a true honor of love and fortitude in its place. With God, the opportunity to meet in a secluded manner is a gift. It allows your heart to embrace the hour to expect God to perform a miracle where you and He meet. The bond is grafted in the manner of true commitment and hope. Seeing the Father perform in you a knowledge where He is the Creator, and the benefactor of all that is good is a sign you have mastered the understanding God is greater than you or I.

The power of the Word is a gift that holds the spirit in the palm of the Lord's hand. God does not harbor a heart; He embellishes it with hope. He is a caregiver whom we can trust. His match and flame burn with intense heat that grafts the spirit and mind to Him. The battlefield of today's life is ever before our hearts and mind. God offers to build within our parameters a boundary where faith and love connect. In this process, we are granted a serene way of life. It is because of grace that all man can know God. God ordained man as His gift to Himself. Man is love to God. However, because of our fallen nature, we fall short of the glory of God. All of man must be redeemed. This process is due to Jesus and His blood being shed strictly for the care of man. No other animal is granted this hope. God may gift one with the desire for animals in his life, but there is no scripture to support mammals or fish inheriting the kingdom of God. God does know our heart, and He may offer this in the form of eternal graciousness, but we alone do not know the detail of this matter. The formula for salvation is in God's message of the blood upon Calvary. The divide between man and God is wide.

The blood Jesus shed is powerful in that it breaches the stalemate and gives it a repair job. By God's favor, we inherit the gift once an admittance of unity with Him is declared. Without this measure, we are lost without eternal life in the arms of the true King. Would the look of love be any clearer? God's favor is solid and manifests as a power where grace is applied and made perfect. Our desire to come to God is not enough. We must adhere to the way God perfected the process. Our admission that Jesus is Lord and we are not is what is required for grace to be applied. If you never accept Jesus as Lord or recognize Him as the living sacrifice, you will not inherit the joy or revelation that God is real.

God the Father never leaves a person in doubt. He is always precise with His directive. His care carries with it the hope of more intent where balance is focused on His person. You will gain the thought process of true measure, and in the process, a commitment of faith will be applied. Care from above is grounded with opportune, magnetic character. God alone is the Waymaker. With Him as the lead, your will shall align, and you will be granted favor. The decision to honor Christ breaks the bond of dark anguish. Your insight develops a pure intent, and the goal of truth unfolds. Take the Word and apply the principles to your daily life. In turn, knowing who is favorable in your sight will graft to your heart, and you will engage with a clear mindset. You won't feel abandoned, and you will not lose face. The market for abundant hope is ever before our hearts. Trust the Savior and know the kinship He has to offer. You won't feel neglected and won't harbor ill will toward another. The pain of intent will dissipate, and new hope will fill its void. Understand God cares about every detail of your life. Even the smallest thing. Your care is what brings Him to the throne on your behalf. Christ carries your burdens and unleashes a power where love meets vain hope and cleanses it whole.

The keeper Himself is wise and prudent. He is not dark or a figure of hatred. Through Him, you are kept free from harm. Although a time for heartbreak or misfortune may befall you, God will never leave your side. He will offer you hope with a clear outlook that He is in control. Pain may ensue, but in the face of discomfort or burning sensation, God the Father is ever at your side. He will lead you to a place of comfort through it all. If you favor a walk with God, you will learn He is compassionate. He is solid in His statement to the heart. Through His leadership, one realizes that He alone is a Master and caretaker in all He does. God's witness is right and strong. When you invest in His person, you gain the perception and growth to obtain a better standard and direct intake of who God is as a person and leader. God may hold the knowledge you desire to move ahead with a plan where your goal is achieved. God is always prudent. He crafts with care a desire to better your logic with a hold on the notion that you may achieve a balance with love and hope, alongside the step of faith He desires for you to take. God is ever faithful. He does not abandon you when the chips are down, nor will He step aside and watch you lose a sure foot. God admonishes the mind and decorates the spirit with prudent uplifting desires and goals. If you feel forsaken, take the Word of God to heart. He will lead you where you need to learn, and the words will come alive. There is power in the verses, and each one is a master all its own. Holding onto the way of God is a straightforward and honest way of being. You can't find faith without looking to God for the bond in which you and He are a team. God alone offers a faith where hearts are united and tethered to the cross. Jesus is the true King, and in Him, we realize that all good comes from His person.

God is the way; the light through Him is how we glean understanding. He is a Master and a caretaker with whom we are always safe. The work of God may not always come in the form of a unity of the mind. It takes effort to read God's word and build ones faith. Seeking God is not effortless. One must apply the principle of a standard in which he knows God is righteous and that He is personable. Look to God to instill the needed gift of knowledge when you read His Word and dine on His instruction. Careful study brings into play the honor of knowledge that strikes a chord and rears a thought process chained to the mind of God. You will grow and learn who the Lord is and how He operates. With knowledge from God comes the clear motive to move with care, and a ministry of love will unfold. You will enhance your heart and be grafted so that you lean into God the Father and unite in spirit with His person. Allow God the honor of feeding from the trough of clear hope. This correspondence transpires when action meets a plan of intent that is pure and honoring in its nature. A ride in the forest proves worthy when the flowers are seen at the base of the meadow otherwise absent from view. In this fashion, God supplies the needed, grafted material that breeds faith and leaves a mind in order. A walk-in faith is subject to the thought God alone is the Waymaker, and He is the one to graft your heart to His. If you rejoice in the fact God is faithful, and He serves His people well, you will glow with the knowledge God can be trusted. The person of God is not one of a shallow body. His character is a guide for all man to aspire to. God will lead with a clear mindset in which you will know His favor holds you close. Even when you are faced with a trial, God is present. His way is to guard and supply reprieve. The token of care offered from His hand is just and whole in its leverage of the heart to His. All God offers is adequate and holy. God is gracious and smooth with an ability to extinguish the dark and bring to light the needed grafting that supplies all to the man who trusts in His character. The Word shows man who the nature of God is. You gain insight, and a clear mental display comes forth. The continuation of growth in knowledge through the Word God has granted us to know Him will bring into play an opportune mental outlook that heals the heart and offers it hope. No one is ever without a shield when God is the caretaker and the one of trust. Our opportune, mental gain is reflective of the spirit of the Lord when we apply a dose of hope toward His manner and forthright presentation of unity.

God is wholesome and true with a reflective nature that offers hope to all and a path with light. The God of man is ever faithful with opportunity at a window of growing grace. If you prefer the dark of the hall and reject the light of the mind, you will never understand the good the Father holds for you. You will be lost in a fog and feel rejected by His person. God is ever faithful. He leads with a unity that offers the mind peace. When you encounter a dark measure and question where it comes from, know God is not the one enacting the cause. He is always just. He does not inflict harm, nor will He advance a loss to your person. Satan is the one who designs missteps and hardship. He is a liar, and he sets up a person to fall. Even if it appears the dark wins on occasion, know this is not true. All things work for good for those that love the Lord. Bounty can be had outside of faith in Jesus, but it is short-lived. A season comes then it retreats. During this time, a growth process is seen where the mind grants favor to either God or rejects Him and leans into sin. An alarm will sound in the person who is being led astray. The strength and hope the man carries within determines whether it is heeded. Following the person of Christ leads to a way of unity and craftsmanship that allows for a solid path forward. When darkness is present, a loss will ensue. Whether in the form of material despondence or mental fatigue, a formula of doubt will be present, causing the mind to reflect on the cause for the indignant manner that ensued. God offers freedom and hope. He does not tie the hands or lengthen a dowery. He is careful and prudent with a loving manner. When He speaks, the heart knows His person is gentle yet influential in a manner of true courtship without an obstructive attachment. God will instruct with care and love, and you will be strengthened. If you feel attacked and alone, reach toward the truth. Look at the holy Word of the Bible and be refreshed. There is power connected to God's book. It is real and holds a frame in which the mind can be sanctioned with the true motive of outward faith. Looking at others and seeing how they speak is a character sign of who they follow. A man cannot offer another a good deed free of fringe benefits unless God leads him. Many think riches are what makes the world go around. This is false. God is the Waymaker. He is the reason man exists. You can run and hide but know God sees and understands every thought you have. He will not turn away when you need Him; He will stand at the helm to direct you and lead you back to the comfort of His arms. Little gestures of love can be found when you look at who carries your thought process. If you allow the Father the gravitational pull your heart has been called to, you will be refreshed and unwind any foothold the enemy has upon your spirit. Casting away a black being will enlighten you to the good God offers, and He will speak clearly. Each moment to study the Word will offer skills and balance with love.

God is prudent. He can control all of life's goals in the form of bonding of the heart. God moves in a clear reprieve, and He opens the sign of truth to the connected bounty your heart desires. When God is working, you will know a cause that is right and just. You will be led in faith, and you will work toward the goal of good measure. If your heart has trouble accepting the Father, you will struggle with the knowledge He offers to you. Being a faithful follower enables the mind to assume God is right and pure. God's word gives enlightenment as to who the nature of God is. The stories written lead us to know that God can perform in an orderly manner. He never strays from the bond He holds and graces the ritual of accord to meet His way of being. God the Father is grace with a gentle manner where you hold His perspective if truth is applied to your heart. God's person is holy and righteous. He is never dark or hurtful. With Him as your lead, you will find your mindset is that of good nature and solid truth. You will limit the gray in your life and seek the light. All steps to a bright future come from the true worship of God alone. All outside influence is secondary. The caretaker of man is ever faithful with a mind of true strength. He does not falter or step negatively. With God, you will grow to love others and find you are blessed when you dine on truth. Your leadership in faith will transpire in realistic forms for others to gain insight and follow suit. The time you spend in honor of the Holy One will offer a gain in direction where your mind is at ease. Even if the wind blows a storm in the direction of your mind and heart, your recollection of the written Word will prevail. You will have the power to combat the negative and extract the doubt hovering within. God pursues the mind and gives it strength. He is opportunistic. His favor is rich and clairvoyant. He knows the inner parts of all man. The heart can be deceived, so gain knowledge and learn how to combat the faults you may carry. Trust the Savior to enhance your perspective and to teach you good measure. His Word will lift up your thought process and graft a special unity that is supplied in strength. You won't be forsaken or cast aside in times of trouble. God will host you to Him. His care never fades.

Today's market is fast and fruitful but man-made. The harbor holds the goods on ships that stow away much in the way of supplies. Without the process of travel and harvest, no goods would be manufactured. There would be a supply and demand issue. Without the hope of a Savior, the world would crumble and be cast aside and forlorn. God is what makes the stand a solid endeavor. Because of the fruit of the vine, man has the opportunity to meet the Son of man. This is God's Son, Jesus. He is the Waymaker. Without Him, what would be the purpose of life? Where would hope lie? Could there ever be a more beautiful picture of grace and love? God has the power to prove who He is in a simple manner of strength, but He has chosen for man to express whom He desires as His God. He allows man to invest in what suits his own heart. Many realize the opportune gift God had bestowed upon man. They know who God is personally, and they invite Him into their daily walk. God does not carry a stick and exact punishment against anyone who has chosen outside of Him. He simply refrains from infringement on their personal choice. God will not enact an attack and won't push His way in. He is gentle and kind. He grants all man the choice to know Him, but He does not impede a line in the sand concerning the option of grace or when it expires. The choice of accepting the King as Savior is ever present and available. Man is the one who chooses on his own accord whom he will serve. What must be realized is no one knows the limit to this decision. There is a point when the heart has rejected God in his final hour. God holds true to the will of man in that He never obstructs the heart's desire. God will grant your request if you walk away from the light and desire the dark. He does not want you to be separated from Him, but free will is a gift He has bestowed to all. How you direct your thought process determines the path you will adhere to. Trusting the Savior is what brings His person to you. If you harbor a life of self-control, you won't relinquish to God the trust required to accept Him as Lord. God is the Waymaker. He knows those who have stepped into the fire of refinement. Redemption is a ministry in which man's control is relinquished, and accepting that God is better proves vital to replacing entangled doubt. Your goal may be to obtain the Lord as King and be a member of His bride. In this is the acceptance that your shield of self-preservation must be forsaken. Only then can one truly dine on the fact God alone is the Master. His greatness is truly what must be recognized. Trust is the key for man to gain his freedom, and with it comes the final measure that God is one and all in all. You are complete when God is the way of your heart. When He is the one you believe in and believe is real, you will accept His way is best. You will surrender your heart and relish the fact God takes care of those who love His person. No other can compare.

A man's temper is guided to be still when the Lord influences His thought pattern. Christ is holy and magnificent. He is true and honorable. In Him is beauty and hope. If you follow the Lord and seek to know Him, the favor He offers will grow and flourish. In Him, a true manifestation of light is ever present. The caretaker of love ever prevails against the wind of hardship. God is a faction no man can comprehend. The Word decorates our hearts and breeds a sworn good measure into the flesh where all faith resides. If you tarry concerning whom to follow, you may lose the Father's will for your life. You may embark on a path that is dark but not seen to you. Your eyes will be clouded, and there will be no light. Look at how God operates and teaches moral, contrite mannerisms. The hollow, dark endeavors slip into the past, and in its place, we discover the real destination of love. The Caretaker is triumphant. It is man who holds a vain interpretation of the Lord. If one does not apply his person toward the King by engaging in scripture, he will not gain the lucrative sight from the Father's hand. Reading the Word and a prayer ministry blossom when grace enters the program. God offers man an outstretched way to close the gap between him and the Savior. The bridge of love the cross holds can be described as a true balance of freedom in which all life is obtained. Without God, one does not recognize their own demise.

Staying committed to the reading of hope carries with it a maternal, heartfelt life in which man accepts his counterpart as an equal. We alone are not capable of loving our brothers and sisters in a manner that is justified. Caring about the life of another is faultless. People reach the goal of enlightenment only when they hear the Word of God revealed to their person. This corresponds in a manner of good intent that transcribes God's wisdom to the realization that He is real and true. The knowledge of courtship between man and his God is clear if the application meets the consistent indwelling of guardian faith. Our witness replicates the love of the Father that He stands ever faithful with true desires of goodwill. Our goal should be to embrace His light and dine on the fact that He presented His Son to act as a salvation for all mankind.

> *For God so loved the world that he gave his one and only Son, that whoever believes in him shall not perish but have eternal life. For God did not send his Son into the world to condemn, but to save the world through him. John 3:16-17 NIV*

Message Seven

God Lights the Path of Man

When a person offers another the hope of who God is, they have invited the knowledge they hold to be shared and witnessed as truth. God incorporates love and grace in the heart, and both receive instruction. Through the process of unity, we grow in favor of the truth. The real motive of our knowledge is the insight we glean and then build upon. If you work for a tyrant but have faith he will change, you are separated by the knowledge that man can learn and be enhanced by the Savior. A solid, opportune method of discovery can be applied toward the work of another in the hope he will bond and form a unity with Christ. Our hearts receive the light when we acknowledge God is real. This formulates the honor that gives the open door for God to move within your spirit. Inviting Him to further your aptitude comes in the form of trust and prayer. This motion brings into play the magnet where faith resides and holds our hearts at a standstill in God's direction. Reading what God has foretold brings the connected bond where we meet God. If you fail to adjust in this manner and impede the material network of you and He, a seed will have been planted but won't take root. No fertile ground will be established in the manner of growth and opportunity. You may accept God is real, but the knowledge of who He is will never come. You will coast believing faith is all you need, but without relationship faith, there is simply the knowledge He is real. The Word of God is faithful in its own right. Just as God builds a bond with those who pursue Him, he steps forth when insight is requested. This action is proven when the Word of God is read and applied. All the motive of good intent does not bring with it a pattern of faith. Many will find they have lost the connective spirit when hardship or misfortune enters their lives. Tackle with intent the living Word of God. It reads as a love letter from Him to all who have been called by His name. No one can escape the judgment that is to come. Only those who have pursued the favor of the Lord will be accepted into His home. Would you let a stranger reside in your care and provide for him eternal goods? Would you not require payment as recompense, so there was a mutual gain? God the Father desires your commitment of love. Through this gift, you gain all eternal rewards. Your bounty will measure beyond belief, and your soul will dine on the gifts of the spirit. An attachment will be crafted where you never lose sight of Jesus as the Savior.

Looking to gain hope outside of faith in God is futile. God alone is the one to offer a plan of salvation where one is secure through the final stages of life. If an infant is captured before birth, would God not favor him? Would God hurt the unborn simply because the mother is the carrier of the physical body? God assures us He is faithful and just. A child is innocent until they reach the age of conception. Their knowledge must reflect a mature stand and hold the mind intact. Grace is ever present in knowledge and truth. God has factored in the mind and the heart. He considers the history and the motive of a man. A child before birth has not been sentenced to the hardship of this world. He has not been convicted of a crime where blood needs to be applied. His history is that of ignorance. He has not been subject to the darkness of sin as he only knows the womb and its secure surroundings. The heart has not been adapted to the knowledge of how to do wrong. The protection lies in the fact God is faithful. He honors a life before its birth. He sanctifies His good measure and adds His grace. It is applicable to one who loves unconditionally.

Once birth has ensued, the mind harbors ill will in the form of sinful nature. It explores the path of good and evil and determines which direction it will pursue. Our intent is what carries us over the threshold. If a villain never steals but harbors ill repute, he is by fault his own best enemy. Coveting another's life or goods brings sin in the form of greed and lust. These reflect the mind and heart. God knows the true motive of every person on the globe. He is a caretaker in whom all will find solace only if they accept Jesus as the real Messiah. A child born with no understanding of who God is cannot be held accountable for his thought processes. Once the introduction of favor has taken shape, the rule of integral faith has taken form. The bounty is determined by the mind and its gravitational pull to either hope and light or dark, intrusive manners. A tidal wave drowns much of the coast, but rebirth transpires, and a new body of life is formed. God's action of faith is subsequent to the acceptance that Christ is Lord. Teaching a young person to trust in the name of the Most High grants the knowledge that God is real. With growth, the mind questions and deceives the heart. Allow children to learn who Jesus is; even if you falter in your explanation, the truth will be revealed. God will honor the fact the message was put forth, and He will extract a plausible recall when the child grows and learns more of the truth.

The trust a person expresses is solid when God is the focus. Man can vary in the goodness he offers. A plan of study shows work at its core. With God, the reading manifests and grows. It is sound judgment to offer your skill set in the way of the Lord. He will show favor and offer in return more of Himself. With that comes the ability to absorb His will and understand His hopes and dreams for you. A shelter provides care in the way it protects the body from harm. The branches of a tree also give coverage, but a wood plank is sufficient to build a barrier where your body receives a patrician against the elements. The structure you support is what will organize your thought process and build within a learned mental graft that lifts the body and its core into the grace of God. A solid way to embrace the King is by prayer and fasting. Through this process, a love of God is enhanced. This application should be practiced and adhered to on a regular basis of commitment. Taking into account medications, one may need to offer as a fast a simple form of unity to remove an indulgence the heart desires. You don't have to refrain from food or drink to honor the King. Any offering you submit in His direction will be recognized. Christ is a Waymaker and a true discipline of love. He crafts the spirit to organize the love He offers and formats the design with a unique gift of hope. The bond between Christ and His people is clear and motivational in the order of good measure. God does not fall victim to a lie or false repentance. He is solid in all He does, never needing to embellish upon a repeat or a do-over. God knows the needs of all man. In Him resides the name of every person ever born or unborn. He does not forget the abortion factor. The babies aborted are also His gift of love. They will be well cared for by the Savior just as any who are birthed. God's entanglement of the love triangle between man, Himself, and the Holy Spirit is a sanctimonious union. It cannot be broken. The river of love God holds is firmly planted with no leakage or driftwood.

God will enhance your unity, and He will embellish upon it in the form of conquering fear or heart loss. The railway is sound when the track is clear. God has vision and care, so no debris ever forestalls the train of His greatness. Look at the Savior and realize He is the epitome of God's character at its best. He refrains from heartache and mischief. He does not injure the mind nor impute a loss of deliverance to His person. He is ever grateful for all who come His way. Your walk should reflect His personage. A day of Christ's love far surpasses the witness of a lie. Cater to the King and be glorified in His manner. You will then learn real commitment and faith.

As the deer pants for streams of water, so my soul pants for you, O God. My soul thirsts for God, for the living God. When can I go and meet with God? Psalm 42:1-2

The star of heaven does not fade nor lose its glory. For God is the real creator of all things right and true. He is glorious in all He does. He crafts with care and supports the ecosystem. He is always binding hearts to His person. He conceals the mind with a flare but never harbors a grudge. He is superior and supported by His Word. When faith is a staple, your mind will engage with the King, and a moral ability to uphold the standard of man against the warrior of doubt will ensue. The power of Christ in a person's life always sustains him. God is not far from His people, nor is He a Waymaker simply for self-gratification. He builds with His people so they may enhance one another. The gift of love is found in the pages of God's Word. It is direct and offers a new lead of information each time it is read. The sights and sounds of this planet do not compare to the beauty God contains in His heart. The world isn't big enough to contain all of what God holds within. If you apply your mind to reading scripture, you become acquainted with the one who built you before you were born. Knowing God personally is a manifest of character as well as sound judgment. Going in the forward direct path of light gains the mind the limited ability to maneuver in a manner of good will. You won't lose your way if you accept the Savior as Gospel. In Him, the creator of doubt must flee. Where God resides, there is His perspective. A unity of great power is encased with each secret meeting of the heart. Prayer is required to gain the important balance that God alone hears our hearts and that we cannot fulfill our goal of unity with Him on our own. He desires all man to know Him personally. He does not step aside when you pray. You are drawn closer to Him. Fear is a manager of a dark interlude. It is not real but a feeling that will flee when you pursue the King and His magistrate in faith. The two work together as a team. Neither is above the other.

Christ was in the picture before the creation of the world. He stood with the Father and built the world and the universe. The two operate as a gift to the spirit because they know our hearts. Their care is unforetold. They alone will grant favor when you apply your heart and mind in their direction. They cannot separate, and they never would desire to. Plant your thought process within their palm and know a balance like never before. Your mind will steady, and you will encase your trust in their person. The favor shown you will enhance, and you will be set free from worry. The truth of the Word is sacred to the action bestowed upon them when recited. Reading aloud grants the knowledge that you aren't afraid to witness the truth. It speaks into the heart of God, and it restores faith. A bond will form, and you will know an alarm of good truth. Favor comes in the silent reading as well. God knows the heart when it is in His Word. One is not greater than the other as long as you profess the King is real and Lord over all you do and own. Shower your faith in the direct path of God. He will carry your heart and acknowledge your mindset. He will adhere to you physically, and there will be restoration. You can gain a perspective of love as well. The things God offers are glorious. They are secure in Christ, and they serve Him well.

Along with our enhancement, God gifts our person and our thought preparedness. He never strays away, so you won't lose the connection even if you disappear into the sunset. God is ever waiting to receive your gift of love pointing to His Lordship. Unity of the soul is captured, and all grace from above is poured upon the person who supports God as Master. Dine on the integral alignment of the Master and His Son. They alone are the bridge to freedom. Only in them can we hope to have appeasement on judgment day. Our will is all that comes between us with God. Surrender it to the one who can apply it toward grace, for there is no other way to eternal love and the hope of life ever after. Seeking to know God gives the mind a clear vision of where hope centers. A triangle ensues, and God the Father, His Son, and the Holy Spirit lead and guide. The unity they offer is grand and superior in makeup. Without this threesome, a vital package of dignity will not exist. You must accept all three and be directed by their intellect and goodwill. Shower your mind into their path. Let nothing great or small be a hindrance to the body or spirit. The unity you desire is there for the taking. The craft of goodwill is ever-present. The body of believers knows this as truth.

Connect with them and gain knowledge from their hearts to yours. Not every believer applies fully toward the goal of enhanced learning. So be selective in your search. Follow suit and start your program of intellect, and repressed desires of care will begin to blossom. You will acknowledge the Master has performed of good measure when you taste the life of a faithful follower. The care package you behold is none other than true grace. Your heart will cause others to claim Christ as their own, and you will perpetuate a more solid statement of faith. Once an incline is formed and you regularly bond, your heart will quickly request more of God Himself. You will taste the good measure and believe with a faith that is solid. No more will fear overrule your thought process. There will be clarity, and a reflective gain of material instinct will ensue. God the Father will build a magnetic pull, and others will see His face displayed within your spirit. Grace is a measure where God intervenes and performs His magic. It transpires from good character and a vision of true Lordship. Work with faith as a backdrop. It is the glue that holds the heart connected with the trust required to secure the mind. When you feel a tug toward the dark, engage in prayer and scripture reading. It will broaden your outlook and put you on the path of truth. A lighted pathway will fill the void, and the dark will flee. A true worshipper grants favor to others, sharing the knowledge that God is who He says He is. Sharing a commitment uplifts the body and incorporates the unity God desires to see. Each character builds upon the other. No one is ever more valuable than the next person. God will use your talents and gifts in a manner that brings Him joy. He lifts man forward when hope is cast His way. Trust God to offer you many goals and joys of the heart. He is a Waymaker whom you may trust. Collecting dust on the wares God provides is not reflective of His nature. Bestow to others the needed reprieve or subsequent entitlement in which man has his needs met by the body of Christ. We are to offer hope and a way forward in growth. God will deliver and meet us through the process. A clear understanding of how to offer help can be performed in many options. There is the witness of work where one performs for a wage. Do this to the glory of God. There is the goal of riches for a better bank account. Keep this without the negative attribute of self only. Also, we can offer spiritual aid. You can entertain in your home or offer a class of instruction for a career path. Encouragement is what the Lord delights in seeing His people offer to one another. It is the backbone to enhancing the heart and mind for both the giver and the receiver. In this active manner people unite and work as a team. Even a phone call of love can be an aide. A gentle reproof even speaks of encouragement. It points a mind in the direction it should go if a fall is about to be presented. These manifestations of the heart all offer an opportune method of great witness. You can build a body up by exerting a care step toward one another. If you focus on building a fraction of goodwill, you will entertain a greater relational hope for another's heart. People live in fear when they have no other to engage with and trust. Pointing someone to the Lord gives them a move in where they begin to search for truth. The hour of hope will be presented, and a clear development will ensue. If a heart is willing, a connective unity begins to form. Giving of yourself ensures others that God is at work on their behalf. His character is displayed, and trust is formed.

The temptation of man to offer only small helpings of unity to one another is in itself a deceptive lie. The more one enlightens the mind of others, the more the bond of faith begins to grow. A caregiver often connects with his patient in unity that offers a partnership of grace. Each factor of love granted from the hand of an operative shows value to another. If you intend to display the love of the Father, you will pursue a life of good measure. You won't abide in the deceptive nature of lying or pleading the fifth during an encampment of a time of need. The Holy Spirit touches the heart and mind and draws a person to His being. This sets in motion the pathway for man to invest in another through the will of God. Time spent in worship brings the mind closer and grafts the body to the living God. The power the Lord holds is translucent. He is righteous and proven to be good. If you invest time with His person, you gain in the way of a mature dinner with each meal you digest. Food of the spirit comes from a grafted bond with the Leader of the world. Who better to trust than the power that created all? God invites all mankind into His presence. He does not subjugate a negative understudy for just a few.

His plan is for all to know Him personally. Though many decided not to follow the ever-present offer. Liking the personal gain to that of a ministry is how God operates. Each detail crafted in the manner of hope and guidance clearly shows that God is the King. He organizes the heart and disperses with it a new offering of love. If you meet God at His throne in prayer, the connection brings a bond where life is eternal. Taking the bond as sacred secures the position God is all-knowing and greater than life itself. The bond of a servant to his master is an example of the relational desires man has toward God. God teaches all of man is subject to His leadership though not a slave to Him personally. Our love of God is enhanced with the presence of His Son Jesus in our lives as a whole. The witness of God is never dark or disruptive. Due diligence is what brings us closer. Reading the Word of God will deliver your mind into the grace of His will. Hosting a family get-together often brings turmoil in the way of hurt feelings. If one applies the salve of God's love to the wound, a bountiful realization that God is ever our Savior comes into our mindset. We then gain hope and a thought process where God is faithful to our hearts. He does not inflict pain or depraved manners of doubt. His care is forthright and solid. It is sturdy and bound by His desire for us to know Him on a personal level. With Christ, our disposition gains a reprieve, and we heal in the manner of love. The worship of the King displays the desire to grow in love with His person and to know Him better. This creates the bond of true kinship with unity at its core. Never doubt God is real. Look at how He developed the mind and its thought process. We are free to disclose our thoughts or keep them private, but God knows them all. In Him are the benefits that man is weak and in need of a Savior. Because of the cross, man can relate to God and build a relational hope where he always has a partner. Many feel God has deserted them. He is the power that trains our hearts to relish His Lordship because we know it is good and fair. No other witness is as strong. God's grace is a bridge where man meets the Maker and is united in His care. God never desires free will to be overrun. He abides in the fact man desires choice. His care is limited to our acceptance that He alone is the Waymaker. Justified thought processes blossom and bloom when the Savior is the center of our being. God alone offers a plan of salvation. No other gains the means to build a better forefront or occupation. God has devised the best maneuverable, opportune mechanism to gain entry to His kingdom. It is by Him alone that the door is open to our salvation. Our actions prove trust. Deception is not hidden. It is revealed upon judgment. In Christ, hope resides, and His love for man is eternal. Dine on understanding and know God favors all who come to Him personally of their own free will. God, the caretaker, is unique. He is set apart. The witness is solid and true. No other holds esteem in the perspective of greatness that God does. He is eternal with a goal for man to be His partner for all time. God the Father is our friend as well as our lead. He is genuine in offering the love He holds to all, no matter how great the sinner is. A light of hope is ever present in His sight, and He delivers the crown of truth when you connect with His spirit. You can't go wrong when God is on your side. You will follow the light if you accept God's guidance written in scripture. Man does not know a timetable of when Christ's return is due to happen, but the Father has given us signs to recognize when it is close. If you see the world crumbling, know the time is near. By the power of grace, you will understand the call is close. We will be lifted up to the heights of heaven, and our faith will carry us to heaven's gate. By the power of prayer and a witness to the fact God is our all in all, we have set the course to be His child forever.

Message Eight

God is the Magnet of Love

The heart of man is different in how it presents itself to others. The goal of most men is to gain employment of the spirit for self-gain. A warrior of God is relational because he cares about whether a person has met the Savior. The goal of a believer is for all to know God personally. When the hope of redemption is presented, it becomes the desire of the heart to receive this gift. God has designed man to offer himself the hope of God through the salvation message. Without the cross, the void is never filled. You will always search for what God designed Him to be within your spirit. There will come a need to know Him personally. He will draw you to Him. Even those who say they never felt God speak are liars. He offers Himself to all of man. He does not pick and choose who is best or last. It is up to our desire that brings forth the mature adaptation of love found by the profession of God as Lord. Every individual knows that serving God is for the betterment of their being. Though many believe to trust a God they cannot see is foolery. It doesn't change the reality that God has offered His gift to them in a manner where they were witness to His presence. He speaks with a clear, mental dialog and offers man His gift of truth. Whether we decide to embrace our Lord is entirely up to our mental desire. Many find God inviting and hopeful. They believe He is the Waymaker and feast on the understanding that God will draw them close. A fish out of water cannot swim back to the pond, but the help of man can restore him to a waterhole where life can be uninhibited. God is that helping hand. He is the provider and supplier of grace, where we meet Him at the throne of goodwill. All God offers is right and true. A plan outside of His character is false. It leads to a dark entanglement where you lose footing and fall to the ground unaccompanied. The liar of doubt and dark understanding holds on to a sinner and enacts revenge. He does not offer real enhancement, only deception, and false approval. God's power holds a unique ministry where all He does is golden and right. God never leaves a fallen soul to flail about in loss and despair. He will enter the scene and offer a reprieve. It is up to the individual whether grace is applied. Repentance must play a role, or all is for naught. A contrite heart seeks approval from God above, and he will leave his sinful state and exact a perpetual balance toward God in the hope of renewal and newfound strength. The deceit of the heart is a false witness. It is not true, nor can it reflect a love of purity. If you feel rejected in the manner of faith, you haven't found the true God of the Bible. Seek His person and gain insight. Applying your thought process brings to the surface your will of good or the desire for ill gain. Targeting the mind of another to offer a lie is deceptive and harmful. God will silence the enemy's goal and bring to the forefront His power and reprieve in the form of love and mercy. The triangle of faith between man and God is what binds the love of God to a person in need. God will entangle the heart and offer it truth. He will lead with care and offer the line of true courage. God is the Waymaker. He is focused and right with a plan of future instruction. He is always on board when a person surrenders their spirit to His will. A recognized loss may ensue, but a lie is the result of the pain. Craft with care whom you choose to pursue. Not all are worthy in their state of decay. A bride wears white to represent the good she feels toward her God. All have fallen in the stand of life, so all need a reprieve, the saving grace of the Father through His Son Jesus. We all will know the true nature of God in its fullest upon judgment day. The time is now to pursue Him in faith. Let Him give you the hope to strive for a better engagement with His person. Care is a friend when Christ is the reason for a goal. The power He contains is beyond measure. All gifts of the spirit unite when the Savior is on the scene. Allow God the ability to bend your will to His. In this action, you will gain trust, and true enlightenment will evolve. God's power holds the key to our witness and love. We are grafted to His person through Him, and our unity is ever before Him. Decide how you wish to pursue your future. It is detrimental to your eternal walk of life. A life of hell will ensue if you choose outside of God. Whether you believe this to be true or not isn't the issue, for all of man know Christ is eternal. All of man understands a walk is needed to survive the holocaust of doubt offered by the enemy. We alone are too weak to build unity with God. He must be the one to act on our behalf. Accept the will God offers as your own and be guided into eternal glory.

God, the caretaker, is right and true. None escape the power of His law. He is eternal and right. His character is not forlorn. He does not forsake a believer, nor will He impede the direct link to His heart. God is the supplier of great, eternal knowledge. By Him, all of man is liable in their chosen way. His grace is honorable, but it is not the key to eternal freedom. That alone is determined by man's heart and mind. A little step toward God can bring eternal rewards far surpassed by an inheritance of lies. The glory of the Father is faith renewed. The King is solid. He is ever present, so go to Him on a personal level and gain entry to the throne. By His power, the gate will open, and you will know freedom and a will of God will ensue. God is gracious and honorable. It must come from the heart with a sincere, mechanical, soundproof rating of love.

God is mighty and to be revered. He is forthright and wholesome. Fear is not of God. It is a lie that befalls the mind when doubt becomes present. Look at whom you serve. Is He not mighty and able to crush the blind directives of the dark one? Does God not allow for your strength to ensue with the power of His connected love to you? God offers the heart and mind a path forward in all ways that are true and just. The hour of witness statesman will have a bounty if He trusts the Savior and King. God's care is deliverable to create beauty in that your soul rests in peace. Through the favor He offers, our drive and ambition is tenfold. We leap toward hoping for more in the way of a divine setting in our hearts. You may have riches that surpass a king's, or you may be a pauper. Either way, your standing in the Lord is a position He alone supplies. A tanker is subtle in the water, even at sea. The bounty it carries is massive, and the loot contains wares and goods that others feel the need to have. Salvation is a direct line to the military response the Lord offers for man to know Him better. The craft of God is enhanced when a person dines on the cuisine of life that comes attached with glory for the King. Our heart and mind are in tune with God, and He orchestrates a desire to pursue His strength. Our heart is connected and outlined in the manner of a gravitational pull enhanced by the hourglass if you seek the favor of God. A little care toward another lifts up the connection and secures our heart's booty. We can gain an intellect where our desire is catapulted by the inner theme of a mighty warrior. Our desire will be enhanced, and we will decide God is our true way of being. Favor from the Lord is not a secret to be held at bay. We are to tell others who the King is. We are to encourage those around our heart to absolve the wish for self-gain and step toward love's true kinetic drive. A shoulder to cry on is not the answer to a love triangle of hurt.

Testing our hearts is not who we should reflect on. We need to pursue the great I Am. In Him, we settle the doubt and hurt and release the bond of brokenness through the work of the cross. Because of salvation, our worries can be prosperous in the way they reflect our strength toward Jesus. The nail of harm a misspoken word can bring is a factor of ill repair. Work toward the goal of truth. Let the Lord handle the detail of repairing the need you have obtained through a balance of harmony and a gift of love. Forgetting the reason we live and are supplied in our daily walk is damage before the cross. The blood of Jesus persuades the mind that faith is superior to neglect and that hope conceals the damage brought on by an offering of division. God will restore what has been robbed and direct the thought process into the light. When applied, simple truth reveals God's love for His child, even if that child is you. Trust the knowledge that God has the details all in place. That His support is ever with you, and you hold a measure of unity with His connected spirit. The little a person gains in the way of doubt is not subsequent to the real divine lineage that God is superior and unique in His control. He will offer a realistic maneuver of gratitude in which your heart is seen and heard. God has set the standard. He has enacted the harmony of man to Himself. His care is genuine and wholesome. He never drives away the faithful and true. His support is ever granted when the bond of intellect secures its position in favor of His guidance. Growing in the position that God alone is the restoration needed for any repair of the heart and mind, you learn to hover over His person, and through this act, a wall is released. Your heart absorbs the honor in which you comprehend that the Savior is who benefits your care package. Look at who Christ serves. Is man not the one He desires to connect with? Is grace not offered in the injury and healed by the Father?

To obtain the heart of the King, one must apply the truth that only He can provide in a time of need. God is the one with the power. He is the magistrate who carries the workload and delivers a gain. He will implement the needed salve, and growth of love will ensue. Trusting the King to provide all your needs is a step toward the goal of acceptance that He is real. He is who He says He is, and He is faithful. A story of faith can be foretold, and you will be the one to tell it if you lean into His chest and breath in His good nature. The star of heaven is God Almighty. He alone captures the mind and sets it free. In Jesus, man is delivered to the knowledge that personal gain will be achieved by the saving grace of love. A ministry can then blossom and build unity with the one called love. A challenge can come into play when deceptive motives ensue. Call on the love of the Father for clarity as to why your words or action are negative toward another. If you embrace your true character and let the Lord control your thought process, you enhance the desire to know Him better. His outlook will be the same as the one you possess. God's power is everlasting, and His hold on the heart is steadfast and absorbent. His character is never failing, and He will provide you the goal of true witness in which you reach toward His desire to complete your own.

Maturity brings flavor and a light to clarify the mind. A child may scream and fall to the floor when injured, but the loving hand of God brings the needed reprimand and outlook of a partner who relishes the reprove and sees it as a bonus in character building. You can gain an opportunity when you apply the cross to the message of your heart. It will grow your mindset and offer an insight that speaks of grace to enlist another's gift of unity. God is the timetable of clarity. In Him, you can ponder and approve and learn the support of a nation while gaining a reflective, moral code in which you learn to speak with love and not haste. If a tussle has ensued, bring to the table the correct feature, and display the moral adaptation of unity God intended. If a body is injured, the ointment of clear apathy is a witness that you trust the Lord above all else. Learning to control the tongue is a guide where hope lives and thrives. Talk in a kind and respectful manner when relaying a tale. The goal is to offer insight, not a slanted perspective. When sin transpires, control the urge to harden the mind and soul. You will reflect the King and grant knowledge to another when discussing the battle, you have been party to. Offer hope and a bright understanding to formulate a better perspective where your heart reflects the love of Jesus. Care is given when a person trusts the Lord to right a wrong. Don't act out of haste. Make unity in prayer and supplication toward the Creator. He will graft to your spirit the knowledge of how to proceed. In the event damage is in the wake, gather the front of the wave and spread the Gospel message through your correspondence in another's presence. You will be delivered from shame, and a true benefit of love will fasten to the mind, and you will enlarge the parameter of concern that has come across the table. Cling to the understanding that Christ died for all mankind. He is ever for the reconciliation of spirits, and all who trust His leadership shall gain and prosper. Shouting to the world an injustice does not solve the pain. It does unleash a dark pointed graft in which faith is lost and support is not recognized. Plan for steps of good measure and let God lead your daily walk. You will gain a witness, and trust and favor will come your way. Silence in a time of need is better directed to God above. Let Him be the source of your strength. Let Him drive the cart and lead the horse. He has a path of righteousness, and we are holy when we follow His footsteps. Christ is our head. He is the Waymaker. In Him, our lives gain respect and love for each member of the body. Every man is a sinner. What drives sin is fear or greed. Pride can also cause a misguided step. These factors can be repaired and tossed aside by offering God your cares and worries. He can mend the mind and give it the blueprint to understanding that pain renders heartbreak. If one adheres to the truth of the Word, the gift of love replaces the onslaught of darkness, and light will proceed. Even if a sinner does not repent of the action he produced, God can bring healing to the scene of injury. He will balance the hurt and treat it with care. The unity in Him will deliver grace, and pain will flee. By the power of faith, we gain the instruction that God is our witness and man does not carry our weight. God alone holds our hearts. He alone is the one to bring us the truth. By His power, our minds can mend, and we can be restored.

God is ever-present and holy. By His dominion, man conquers the loss of love in faith. Through His leadership, all man can gain the hope of eternal mastery of the love of God. Focus on His way of presentation. Read what scripture says concerning the faith. Follow in the footsteps of David and know God is ever faithful to pursue you in love.

Hear my cry, O God; listen to my prayer. From the ends of the earth I call to you, I call as my heart grows faint; lead me to the

***rock that is higher than I. For you have been my refuge, a strong
tower against the foe. Psalm 61:1-3 NIV***

The touch of the hand of the minister of great reward is ever before the
love He offers, as well as the gift of knowledge. Through Jesus, man is given
a clear upbringing of nature and her elements. God the Father is caring and
honest. He is not doubt or darkness. With Him, a person finds the peace
needed to go forth and explore the greatness of God. A character of good,
moral faith leads others to truly understand He is real. In this knowledge,
man is granted the ability to move in a faith manner of united bliss. God is
the seal of righteousness.

He is acquainted with all of man. He is not a bystander in that He puts
forth a real cognitive unit in clear mental gain. His decisive manner is of care
and concern. He is not a target of doubt. His way is just with a clear motive
at its core. In hope lies the gift, and true understanding springs forward with
care as a minister along the way. Leadership is not a triangle of deceptive
onslaught if Christ is the one in the lead. Many miss the opportunity to grant
others insight out of fear or doubt that they will lose face. God operates in
the realm of total commitment. He leads with a cause of justice. In His work
can be found the favor all desire and relish. A simple nod in His favor will
supply the necessary faith and standing that offers Him a manner of good
output resulting in a growth of life toward the goal of unity. Never
underestimate that God is genuine and fruitful. With His person as your
backdrop, looking into the heart of another brings a clear, uplifting desire
where all you apply toward a goal is righteous. Plan for your way of life to
be committed in faith with the hope of eternal rewards as your station. The
time frame for man to know God is ever before us. No one knows their final
breath or intake of faith so supply your mind with the realization God will
act on your behalf come judgment day. The matter of unity will be present,
and He will offer the way forward with care. Allow the Minister to reach into
your person and dine on His excellence.

Look at how God offers His love to all. Even the downcast have a home
in His heart. A person's status is secure if they have committed to the King
their patronage. A flower blooms when God declares His glory to it. He
produces wisdom and offers it freely. Simply go to Him in favor and unite

with the cause of good measure, and a plan will formulate. The honor He will bestow will reckon forth a unity, and you will know peace and how to proceed with a clear unit in graciousness. The parallel pardon of the mind to the heart is a measure God responds to when both seek His goodwill. Caretaking is something God honors. If you focus on Christ, your gateway to Him will not be bound. The entry will be secure, and truth will reside. The formula to enhancement brings the bounty of light where man and God unite. With God at the helm, a path of greatness ensues. Even if you walk alone, know God the Father honors your steps of unity with Him. God will judge those who came against you and offer you an honest manner to overcome their affliction. The mind of a believer is that of solid hope.

If you have entertained the option of telling a witness for God and beauty has been brought forth know God the Father is at work. He will decorate the love you offer His way and invest in your goal. He is the Waymaker and King. Through His objective to gain fruit, your mind will adhere to His unity, and you will build with a clear vision. Even when doubt is present, you can harbor a justified field of dreams that will cast away the lie and offer the real light of the soul in its place. God is the builder in whom we find love. All projects of wise counsel begin in the form of hope. If you have stepped forth and done all you know to do, wait and trust God is making a way for a reality to come in the form of good measure. Many find faith a guide in love. With it comes the heart of great expectation. God works to enhance the mindset and deliver a dream when it is pure and wholesome.

There may be obstacles that need attention. Knowing God will alleviate the stress, and in its place will be the desire to pursue the catch with a line and sinker. God favors those who believe He is great. The people He connects with are the ones who show Him respect. He is mighty and giving in the manner of goods and services. When faith meets the desire, a plan will form, and an option will present itself. God will enable your dream to become a reality and guide your directive to meet His. Shoulder the love God offers and witness true connective love. The grounding of a plan will shelter the mind and bring into play the needed measure for it to become a reality. There need not be fear. God the Almighty is a crafter. He understands the workings of all things.

Through His guidance, you can sprout a lot of ideas and make them grow. God offers our hearts the blessing of faith. Dine on it and know a welcome mat of fresh ideas. A party is not complete unless the guest of honor is at the table where fellow brothers and sisters witness his day. Shelter your love and feed it the Word of God. Your witness will thrive, and you will learn a multitude of economics where opportunities abound. Keep your eye on the faith needed to supply the Caretaker with action. In doing so, you will gain the perspective that God's love is far above your own. The knowledge that God cares is what operates in the manner of good measure. Let your focus reward your heart. A balance of unity is found in how we operate as a whole. Take your wisdom to the test. Are you searching for a way to move forward with a plan? Have you surrendered the love you desire to God above? Are you planted in the Word? Are you trusting God will act in a loving manner? If you glue your heart to His person, a knowledge of unity will ensue, and the offering of great mental gain will arise. God can perform on a scale the heart dares not trod. Think about His person and relate to Him in a personal manner. Trust His line of concordance. Let Him be the one to organize your thought process. Engage with Him in prayer and ignite the love He holds for you. God is a lover of the heart. In Him rests the bond we all require. Look in the direction of care and embrace the door that opens. If God favors your desire, it will grow and bloom. If you trust His Word, know He will act, and a bounty will be had. Lead in the fashion of honor and indulge in the heart you hold dear. God crafts with love, and His bond is ever-present. He will lead and direct your spirit, and you will know He has spoken with care. Never feel like your dream is minor or not grand enough. A salute in the way of hope will set in motion the divided bridge, and a steel plate will graft to the mind where you will know the step to move forward. Accept what you do not know but lean into what God offers on a platter of grace. He will include your input and offer a better way. His plan is superb and crafted to meet your goal of ingenuity. The alarm of false pretense will be dismissed, and you will be enlightened to hold the hand of the Most High.

The unity of Christ to another is simple in the order of grace and hope. By His power, man can know freedom. The heart will inherit a unity that grafts it to God, and through the process of salvation, man gains life. The rock displayed in the manner of good measure is a built-in love canal where hope is ever flowing. Only those who trust the Lord will know Him personally. Through the scripture process of reading, an insight is developed and a bounty put forth. The hour of doubt recedes, and a plan formulates. In the care of God, you will enhance the unity by His person attached to you in a significant altitude and display of affection. The goal of all man is to know Him personally; whether faith is present or not, the heart accepts the witness gifted to it by the Lord. The motion of God to His people is a unit of forward passages containing love messages in written form. Look at how the Savior records His love for His people through the message found in Daniel.

> *Daniel answered, "O king, live forever! My God sent his angel, and he shut the mouths of the lions. They have not hurt me, because I was found innocent in his sight. Nor have I ever done any wrong before you, O king. Daniel 6:21-22 NIV*

God is ever one to be present and in accord with the delivery of His great way of being. He does not skate from one bounty to another in the form of doubt or loss. Through Him, the gateway of life floats in care and admonishment to the power therein. Silence of the mind is a quiet reprieve if God is the one at work. A ministry to the making of lineage crafts the ability to further the goal of a direct hope centering on the unity Christ is within us. The favor of the Lord is never removed when trust is built. Look at how man falls each time He steps outside of God's care. When a partner loses his way, does he not need help to return to the table of good measure? Always a bounty of faith, God pursues man because He never slips away without being requested to leave first. God the Father is ever faithful and prudent. His care is equal to none other—a balance of love and human connection blossoms when favor is shown. By the power of God, man is lifted up into the realm of true unity. There can be no other way to move forward with great understanding. Our own interrupted pattern of doubt breeds a center where we do not actually control our minds. God allows our hearts to remain intact through the conversion of grace, which signifies He is faithful and respectful to our wishes. You will learn a bond of love far surpasses that of kinship to the liar of man. Satan is not the one who shows real grace or enhanced opportunity. He will rob and destroy all that He can. Follow the Lord and gain the true witness of gracious power and a real connected drive that performs for the spirit in such a way that glory is given to the King. The mind is cleared through the act of salvation, and a pathway is taken where the desire to serve God is enhanced.

Reflect on your center attitude. Do you invest in the body of the Lord? Are you at peace when another gives you insight concerning how to perform an act of good measure? Do you embrace the hope God will share your gifts and talents with others? Do you lean into God and offer your desires before the throne He attends to? Can you envision time away from His charge? Would you allow a child to balance all he knows and let him be the one to determine a bedtime schedule? God is our counterpart. He is deliberate in all He manufactures and builds. The glory of God is reflective of His person. The sound of love comes to His ears when a person repents and accepts His salvation message as Gospel. The knowledge God is power lifts the channel and brings into the light that the King is justified and a Caregiver. No king ever lived that can do what Jesus has done. Only He is the Waymaker. By the love He offers, all may know freedom and the drive of the everlasting will grace the heart.

Each person who engages in the reading of the Word of God has found faith to meet his will. The factor of life is the connection it holds and garnishes. Look to God for the development of a guided mind. You will gain prosperity and lean into His person, thus enveloping His mind to yours. By the election of a process of grace, we witness the perfect unity of the maker of man. No balm or salve can cure the pain left behind when a person retreats and steps away from the unity of a relationship. Only God can release the doubt of value and offer a grave unity where He is the ointment that heals. Our heart is designed to know Him personally. Through the process of trust, we entertain the connected gateway and believe the true nature of Christ is that of wholesome love. When we understand the Father is here as a standard and a character builder, we relate ourselves to the understudy of turning from sinner to magistrate and lover of the soul. Each character witness should reflect God as a nurturer and true companion. The star of Bethlehem displayed the glory of God. It offered a symbol of unity that guided the watchers to His place of birth, confirming that Christ was born in a manger and not in a palace. A birthplace does not distinguish the mind with a relaxed unity. It is simply the door to witness one life. Understand God the Father offered His Son for all of man. He declared unity in the way He presented

Him to the world. He did not make it a requirement to list the heart and describe it to His person. He desired all of mankind to meet Him in faith and offer their hearts in love as a freewill offering to His person.

Robin Arne believes…

God is the creator of all man. He is the center of our lives, whether faith is present or hidden from view. God alone is the witness to who Christ is. He grafts to our knowledge that He is a benefactor for our soul. In God, we find a mechanism to unify the faith we contain and bring it forth toward the person of Jesus. In doing so, we learn who the Creator and His Son are. With the wisdom found in the Word of God, one can be a scholar, and insight can be built upon. Follow the path of righteousness and pursue the man of Jesus. He is both a friend and a guide. In His care, we learn how to live and move freely without deceptive input from the dark side. The knowledge God holds is unequivocal. Jesus is the way, the truth, and the life. Let Him lead your steps and find beauty where your mind is reconciled to the fact that God is who He claims to be. His power is forever, and He is the Waymaker. Grace is the key to acceptance of His person. Tithe in the form of unity and offer to the King your heart's desire of love in the form of your surrender to Him as Lord. With the gift of this act, all your cares will be cast upon the one who controls the world. The holy, mutual, attained goal will be a witness of good measure. Your enhanced way of thinking will bring into play a motive where others will witness your mark of faith. You won't lose footing or fall into deceptive thoughts. God is real. Let Him lead and develop your character while showing concern for your welfare. There is no greater love or connection of truth. Speak to God and draw Him near. You will find a balance, and a goal of unity will transpire. God's truth is never ending, and in it is freedom of eternal hope.

Robin Rochel Arne

About This Book

This book contains a look at how the Lord builds up an individual and how He enhances his mindset. God offers man the knowledge of how to perform in the manner of faith and hope. By His person, man can blend both truth and goodwill as one. God the Father graces the spirit with unity and a solid undertaking in care. You will learn how to respond when pain enters your heart, and the knowledge will help you grow toward a better mental state when Christ is known as the key to healing. The body of believers can offer hope to those in need. Look toward the goal of a reflective desire to see others gain in the manner of faith. This tool you hold in your hand is insight with character-building properties. A plan of endurance is never bought without a price. Study this book and gain hope that the God of the world is in your corner. He is faithful, and He will grant favor in accordance with the love He holds for all mankind. You are no different. Trust the unity He will provide and elect the power He has available through the message of the cross and its contents therein. Knowledge is a tool where many can find favor. Help all you know to gain freedom in the form of healing. By reading The Hurts Can Be Repaired, you will learn the mind is crafted by God, and He knows the contents therein. His available character teaches us how to mature and discover a better way of living.

The goal of this book is to grant insight as to whom you serve. With the knowledge it presents, your mind will flourish, and you will ignite a passion for the Lord not previously known to you. The messages outlined give care and an opportune way of approaching the knocks that threaten the mind and heart. Be delivered to a goal of liberty. Trust God as your Savior and be set free in the knowledge written herein. The understanding you will gain will flow freely to others, and you will rejoice in its display through you. God cares for all. Be a participant of His care and thoughtfulness. Allow His person to grace your heart and dine on strength.

Robin Arne is available for author interviews. For more information contact us at info@advbooks.com

To purchase additional copies of these books, visit our bookstore at
www.advbookstore.com

Advantage
BOOKS

"we bring dreams to life"™
www.advbookstore.com